The
Colonel Stephens Railways

A PICTORIAL HISTORY

John Scott Morgan

DAVID & CHARLES

NEWTON ABBOT LONDON NORTH POMFRET (VT)

FARMERS' TRAIN

The Kent and East Sussex Line

Ever seen a railway train
wheel deep in the wheat?
Poppies on the boiler dome:
wreaths of meadow-sweet
twined about the driving wheel—
burnished brass and polished steel:
puffs of steam like woolly lambs,
on the line to Bodiam?

His chimney's tall and thin and crowned
with a bell-mouthed top,
brassbound
all round.
He's painted green like new spring grass
and he's always pausing
at the level crossing
to let the farm carts pass.

He sees real trains at Headcorn Halt,
where he's rather shy
as they thunder by
from lordly London to the Coast.
For they're very long
and he's very short,
and he wonders if they give him a thought:
but at Methersham you'll hear him boast
that his very best mate's
the eleven-eight—
the Dover Express that's never late.

But—
as soon as he gets out of sight
of the Main Line with its metals bright
then once again
he becomes THE TRAIN
and there's pride and swank
in every puff, as he goes chuff, chuff,
with a piercing whistle now and then
(Get out of the way, you silly hen)
on his lordly way
to Newenden.

He puffs past farms,
he steams past barns,
to the Biddenden maids he tells tall yarns.
He's a snorting giant
at Freezing Hill,
he whistles the miller
at Northiam Mill,
he puffs the day's news
at the crossing gate
and says what a shame he's
five minutes late!
and snorts of course
it's the Main Line's fault!

He carries grain and he carries hops.
Wherever you hail him, there he Stops!
in fact he's a friendly sort of train.
He takes out shopping farmers' wives:
he carries a load of bees in hives:
and he carries pigs,
and oats
and goats
and several boxes of lollipops
for the village kids
at the village shops.

He knows the Marsh and he knows the Weald,
he-knows each wood and he knows each field:
with his bright green paint
and his glistening brass:
the rabbits stop
to see him pass.
And Arcadia's just another station
on his twice-a-daily
pere-
grination!

British Library Cataloguing in Publication Data

Scott Morgan, John
   The Colonel Stephens railways: a pictorial history.
   1. Railroads, Local and light—England—History
   I. Title
   385'.5'0942   HE3821.C/
   ISBN 0-7153-7544-X

First published 1978
Second impression 1980
Third impression 1985

© John Scott Morgan 1978

Printed and bound in Great Britain
by Biddles Ltd Guildford and King's Lynn
for David & Charles Publishers plc
Brunel House Newton Abbot Devon

Published in the United States of America
by David & Charles Inc
North Pomfret Vermont 05053 USA

Contents

6

Holman Fred Stephens; 1868-1931.

Former LBSCR A1X 0-6-0T No 2 *Portishead* seen here with a train of ex-LSWR four-wheelers at Portishead in 1938 awaiting the road to Clevedon. The WC&PR purchased two LBSCR A1X 0-6-0Ts from the Southern Railway, the first in 1926, becoming No 2 *Portishead*. A second engine was bought in 1937 and became No 4. Later both locomotives were taken into GWR stock, becoming Nos 5 and 6. No 5 survived until 1954 in store at Swindon Works.

Photomatic/Ivor Gotheridge collection

1909   Reconstruction of the Burry Port & Gwendraeth Valley Railway

1910   The Potteries, Shrewsbury & North Wales reconstruction and metamorphosis into the Shropshire & Montgomeryshire Light Railway

1911   East Kent Light Railway

In the same year he also took over the Weston, Clevedon, & Portishead Light Railway from G. S. Newton who in that year emigrated to Canada. After war service in Britain, between 1914 and 1916. when he was given the rank of Lt Colonel, Royal Engineers (TR). In 1920 he promoted the Edge Hill Light Railway. In 1922 Stephens was responsible for building the North Devon & Cornwall Junction Railway, and for taking over the Snailbeach District Railways. In 1922 he was also responsible for the Ashover Light Railway. In 1923 Stephens was offered the chance of grouping his lines into the Big Four. He declined, preferring to remain independent.

After 1923 he was made consultant engineer for the Welsh Highland Light Railway and later the Festiniog; then he was made chairman and managing director of both concerns by the shareholders. This move did not make the workers on both concerns very happy. From the terse correspondence and memos it was clear that Stephens had little time for the Celts on either line, especially those who worked at Boston Lodge works on the FR.

During the latter years of the 1920s Stephens put forward schemes for Light Railways up and down the country; most were to get no further than the drawing board, for example proposed lines like the Isle of Lewis Light Railway and the Surrey & Sussex Light Railway. One line that nearly made it was the Southern Heights Light Railway which was to run between the Southern stations at Orpington and Riddlesdown in Kent. It had the backing of Sir Herbert Walker and the Southern Railway Board. The Southern even put the line firmly on the map by showing it on SR network maps in carriage compartments. The Southern Heights was to be financed with American money and was to have been worked electrically. At the eleventh hour the scheme fell through for two reasons, first the passing of the Transport Act (London) in 1928, which had the preliminary effect of streamlining transport in and around London which made the line surplus to requirements, and second, opposition from the local councils at both towns. Both factors helped to destroy the scheme. It also contributed to the hastening of the Colonel's death which followed after a number of strokes on 23 October 1931 when he was 63.

He owned several properties. In addition to the family home in Hammersmith he owned a house in Tonbridge and rented rooms at Robertsbridge and Dover. He often stayed at The White Hart, Tenterden when visiting the K&ESR. He also belonged to a number of London clubs and professional institutions. His only interest apart from railways appears to have been classical Greek and Roman mythology. This comes out in the names given to locomotives on his various lines, names like *Juno, Dido, Hesperus, Hecate.*

He will also always be remembered for his petrol railbuses and railcars. However, few people realise the prototype was in fact a Wolseley Sidley chassis which was on trial as a rail lorry on the K&ESR before going to the Selsey Tramway as an early petrol railcar.

After his death in 1931 his lines slowly declined into bankruptcy and closure, and a new boss had taken charge of the group, W. H. Austen, who had been a friend and partner of Stephens from the days of the Paddockwood project. Austen was to manage what remained of the group until the government take-over with nationalisation of railways in 1948, after which most of what was left was slowly closed down.

Today little remains of this empire of minor lines. The Southern Region still operates a short section of the East Kent Railway as far as Tilmanstone Pit. Part of the Kent & East Sussex is being restored by a preservation society, and the Festiniog Railway has nearly been fully restored. The Plymouth, Devonport & South Western Junction still carries a BR passenger service between Bere Alston and Gunnislake.

The Colonel and his empire of minor lines have been steeped in mystery and the subjects of many tall stories. This album, it is hoped, reveals something of the truth of the life and works of one of the most fascinating administrators in Britain's railway history.

John Scott Morgan

1 THE RAILWAYS AND THEIR ATMOSPHERE

A tribute to the rural folk who lived on the various Colonel Stephens' Light Railways

The Colonel Stephens' Light Railways: what were they really like? Looking back over the years, through the mists of time, one can imagine the early days of most of the railways managed by the Colonel, before the days of the motor bus and lorry.

The railways he managed possessed something that the main line railway could never hope to have. Indeed the Colonel Stephens' railways had a deeply human spirit that lacked the humbug and hypocrisy of the railway rule book, deeper rooted than any railway official could ever hope to understand, for the world of the large companies was the world of the timetable and the express, of the heavy fitted freight and the suburban train bustling its way from main line terminal to the outer suburbs.

In contrasts from the far north of Wales to the rolling downland of South East England, the Colonel's little rural lines ran between the hills and over the streams and rivers, onward their journey went, often from nowhere to nowhere. They went through some of the most beautiful country that Britain could offer, and as the trains passed along their timeless path, from little stations and sleeper-built halts from dawn to dusk, they seemed to take with them the hopes and the dreams of the country folk they served so well, the same local folk who manned the stations, maintained the track, repaired the fences and operated the trains. Most were village folk, coming from the rural areas through which the Colonel's many light railways ran. They knew a peace and tranquillity so very far from our world of industrialists and trades unionists, for theirs was a world where demarcation did not exist.

The station masters and porters of these country stations were some of the last freemen of Britain, for in most cases they were their own bosses and it was entirely up to them how the railway ran. Not for them was it necessary to refer to higher authority to hold connections at junctions. Moreover, not only did they run their stations smoothly and efficiently, but also somehow found time in their day to tend the flowers in the station garden or give a polite piece of advice to any stranger visiting their domain, so unlike the station staff of many of the stations on today's ultra-modern railway system.

Only a man like Stephens could possibly have run these lines, for he was more than a mere railway engineer or promoter, and so much more than a general manager or organiser. Like an emperor he ruled his empire from his office in Salford Terrace, Tonbridge. His domain stretched far and wide, and his concept of railway operation seemed to exist throughout his light railway kingdom. All the colonies in Stephens' domain seemed to have a great measure of individuality and independence, for although they all had much in common all seemed to have so much individual character in themselves. No two were really alike, and all offered so much to the transport historian and enthusiast who took the trouble to venture off the beaten track to the Rolvendens and Kinnerleys of this rural world. Such a trip would take one almost out of reality and into a time where people were individualists and society valued each and every member by what he stood for in himself, rather than by sheer materialism. One felt almost privileged to be there, but the people of the Kentish Weald and the Welsh Border Country were a friendly crowd, people who in the main one could trust and make friends with. As the train rumbled and bucketed its way through the darkening evening sky, as the gas lamp flickered, casting long dark shadows down the carriage compartment walls, and as the steam of the little Emmett-like locomotive plumed skywards in puffs of pure white vapour, one had a feeling of great contentment, for the day's work was done, and it was time to return to nowhere, from whence one had come that morning.

But then came a war—the second great conflict—and after it was over and all had returned to peace, nothing was ever quite the

same again, for much had been lost and destroyed and people's hearts were hardened and changed. Even in the 1930s buses had already begun to displace rail services on the grounds that they were more flexible, more economic and better suited to the needs of rural communities. One by one the Stephens lines closed. After the war the pace quickened. Then came the Beeching Plan when legislation was used as an excuse to close as many rural railways as possible, regardless of whether these same lines made a profit or not, and regardless of whether the local country folk had an adequate bus service. Today many rural areas including many served by Stephens railways are totally without public transport.

The Paddock Wood & Hawkhurst Railway in its last years, one of several Southern Region branches in East Sussex and Kent closed to passengers during the 1950s and 1960s. Class H 0-4-4T No 31519 leaves Paddock Wood for Hawkhurst in the summer of 1959.

G. M. Kichenside

Below:
Opening day on the S&M with former LSWR 0-6-0 *Hesperus* and train of ex-works Midland bogie carriages posing for a photograph at Meole Brace. The locomotive is seen here in immaculate blue livery. A number of locomotives were painted red for a time. The vehicle behind the locomotive is a Midland four-wheeled parcels full brake. This vehicle was used long after the end of passenger services, often as a brake van.

LPC Ian Allan

The EKR had quite a collection of locomotives and rolling stock which were repaired and overhauled in the workshop at Shepherdswell. At the time of opening in November 1912, the EKR owned an ex-GWR saddle tank, No 1386 as EKR No 1, plus a selection of open wagons, and the K&ESR bogie Pickering brake which was, at this time, used only for inspection work.

The East Kent ordered a new Hawthorn 0-6-0T similar in design to *A. S. Harris*, on the PD&SWJR. The order was placed shortly before the outbreak of the first world war but the engine was sent to the WD, presumably in France, when completed.

Compensation was paid with a Kerr Stuart 0-6-0T, which was sold at cut price to the EKR in 1914. The mainstay of motive power on the line was in the form of SE&CR O1 0-6-0s, although shortly after the war the line acquired two former LSWR tank locomotives. One was the Adams 4-4-2 radial tank and the other the Beattie 0-6-0 saddle tank. In 1916, when passenger trains were introduced, the East Kent acquired an LSWR unrebuilt 'Ilfracombe goods' 0-6-0 locomotive. Presumably this old-timer was purchased because there was nothing else available. The line also had locomotives on loan from the K&ESR from time to time and both *Northiam* and *Hecate* worked on the EKR at different times in their lives.

The carriage stock consisted of vehicles of LSWR, LC&DR and NLR origin, mostly four- and six-wheelers. In 1945, two LSWR brake thirds were purchased from the Southern Railway, to replace most of the old carriage stock already described.

Most of the goods vehicles used over the line belonged to other main line railway companies but the EKR had a small fleet of open wagons mostly used for internal work.

The line managed to carry on through the depression and up to the years before the outbreak of the second world war, during which traffic began to pick up again because of the increased output from the coalfield and the WD also operated rail-mounted guns on the railway; but after the war was over traffic decreased again and the line returned to its pre-war state of quiet inactivity.

Like so many of the Colonel's railways, the East Kent has its tales, some tall, some true. One that comes readily to mind involved a Saturday afternoon train in the autumn of 1945. The train was headed by one of the O1 0-6-0s and consisted of a single bogie brake carriage and a string of empty open wagons plus a brake van bound for Wingham Colliery. The train left Shepherdswell 10 minutes late and proceeded through Golgotha Tunnel and up past Elvington Halt at a somewhat leisurely pace. On arrival at Knowlton Halt, a friend of mine flagged the train down and duly got on. With a lurch the train started again and wended its way towards Eastry. As the train approached Eastry South a fat gentleman came into view, standing by a boundary fence.

The old boy, probably a local fruit farmer, put his hand out, as if trying to stop a bus; by his feet stood four or five baskets of farm produce for market; but instead of stopping as the country gentleman undoubtedly thought it

No 6 and train bound for Shepherdswell near Eastry in 1932. The embankments along this section seem to be made from ash and slack. The carriage on the end of the train is one of the Kent & East Sussex Pickering bogie vehicles. *I. Gotheridge collection*

Left:
Eastry station on the East Kent Railway, looking towards the junction of the Canterbury Road branch curving away to the left and the Sandwich Road line going straight ahead, photographed in 1935.
C. R. L. Coles

would, the train continued its leisurely pace past him, despite his screams of abuse and scorn.

After reaching Wingham Colliery where the locomotive disappeared for half an hour to shunt wagons, the train continued to Canterbury Road, where a very strange thing happened. Instead of the locomotive running round the train, as in the normal railway sense, the locomotive, after reaching the level crossing just ahead of Canterbury Road Station, stopped, uncoupled and ran over the crossing to the station and the carriage, which was just in front of a set of points leading to a siding, was levered into motion with the aid of an iron bar carried in the brake van. After the vehicle had been manoeuvred off the main line, the locomotive made its triumphant return, coupled on to the carriage, and started back for Shepherdswell. Any passenger wanting to get off at Canterbury Road was generally ushered down by way of a ladder or porter's barrow, used as a ladder to the ground at Canterbury Road siding.

As the train worked its way home, around the curve just north of Wingham Town (which was constructed of straight rail laid end to end to form a gradual curve) and past the stations at Wingham Town and Eastry, it came presently to the place where earlier on that very afternoon they had left behind a passenger.

Some two and half hours had passed since the last meeting of the two parties concerned and by now the fat farmer had equipped himself with plenty of home-grown ammunition in the form of rotten eggs, tomatoes, apples and many things from the farm compost heap.

The locomotive crew's joviality changed to dismay, as the train passed this notable gentleman for not only did he have more abuse for them than he had before, but also to match, he had items of a more penetrating nature which he duly hurled at the driver and fireman, scoring a number of direct hits into the bargain.

After the war the mangement tried to smarten the line up. Most of the work carried out involved repairing buildings and rolling stock, a number of old vehicles were broken up for scrap, and several of the locomotives were laid aside at Shepherdswell pending their fate. In 1946, the Southern Railway re-purchased the Adams radial 4-4-2T for use on the Lyme Regis branch. This engine is now preserved on the Bluebell Railway in Sussex.

In 1947 the railway carried on in spite of the forthcoming nationalisation of railways a year later. On 1 January 1948 the line became part of British Railways and things started changing rapidly, for from 30 October 1948 the passenger service over the Shepherdswell-Canterbury Road section ceased.

The EKR was one of the first lines to lose its passenger service on the new British Railways network. More closures followed on 27 October 1949 when the section between Eastry and Richborough closed. The line above Sandwich Road had been derelict for years and had not seen a train since the early part of world war two, when the Army had a rail-mounted gun on this section.

The last two sections to close to all traffic were from Eastry to Canterbury Road on 25 July 1950 and the line between Eythorne and Eastry which closed on 1 July 1951, leaving only the section from Shepherdswell to Tilmanstone Colliery in use, which it still is today.

Top left:

Shed scene at Shepherdswell in 1936, showing locomotive No 6 with its new boiler and No 4 the Kerr Stuart 0-6-0T. To the left is the PW crane and runner, behind which are the frames and cab of 0-6-0ST No 1, formerly GWR 1386.

Photomatic/I. Gotheridge collection

Above:

Former LSWR Beattie 0-6-0ST, EKR No 7, takes water at Woodnesborough. *L&GRP*

Left:

Line-up of motive power at Shepherdswell in 1931. From left to right are: unrebuilt ex-LSWR 'Ilfracombe goods' 0-6-0 No 3 formerly 394, Kerr Stuart ex-ROD 0-6-0T No 4, 0-6-0ST No 2 from the WC&PR, ex-LSWR 127 No 7, LSWR 4-4-2T No 488 (EKR No 5) in front of which stands O1 0-6-0 No 6. *H. C. Casserley*

Right:

Golgotha Tunnel shortly after its completion in 1912, looking towards Shepherdswell, showing the chalk cutting and the tunnel built to take two tracks. This section of line is still in use today for coal traffic from Tilmanstone Colliery. *W. H. Austen TRC*

A double headed train on the EKR consisting of 0-6-0s No 6 and No 3 near Eastry in the early 1920s. No 3, the unrebuilt 'Ilfracombe goods' purchased from the LSWR in 1916, was withdrawn in the late 1920s. This locomotive cost more to purchase than any of the rebuilt Ilfracombe locomotives used on the other Stephens' lines. *Ken Nunn LCGB*

Canterbury Road Station in 1925, the end of the EKR. Originally it was hoped to extend the line to Canterbury City, some 15 miles away. In the distance can be seen the cutting towards Canterbury which was built but never used. Canterbury Road was only a mile outside Wingham Village. *W. H. Austen collection*

Domeless Stirling 0-6-0 No 6 at Wingham in 1932 with a train of former Midland and LSWR six-wheelers bound for Shepherdswell. No 6 was purchased from the Southern Railway in 1923 as SR 372 and rebuilt with an O1 boiler in 1933. No 6 was fitted with a squat chimney to operate through Tyler Hill tunnel on the Canterbury & Whitstable Railway. *Real Photographs*

The pithead at Tilmanstone in 1914, showing a variety of open wagons belonging to various railway companies and private coal merchants. Note the coal loading hoppers and the Tilmanstone open wagons in the foreground. *W. H. Austen TRC*

3 THE ROTHER VALLEY RAILWAY

(Later the Kent & East Sussex Railway)

The Rother Valley Railway started life in 1897, shortly after the 1896 Light Railways Act was passed. The line was the Colonel's fourth project, after the Paddockwood & Hawkhurst line, and his first railway under the new Act. It ran from Robertsbridge in Sussex, on the South Eastern Railway Tonbridge-Hastings line to Tenterden in Kent. The original Tenterden Station was situated at what was later known as Rolvenden, and it was here that the new company built its locomotive shed and repair shops. The railway served the rural agricultural district of the southern Weald, which stretched from the Ashford area of Kent and ran down to the Romney Marsh taking in the Rother Valley with its hop-farming and wheat-growing, to Rye and Pevensey.

The line opened to traffic on 2 April 1900, from Robertsbridge to Tenterden (Rolvenden), and for the opening the Company had purchased two 2-4-0Ts from Hawthorn Leslie of Newcastle-upon-Tyne, Nos 1 (named *Tenterden*, 2420 of 1899) and 2 (named *Northiam*, 2421 of 1899).

In addition to the locomotives the Company ordered a rake of six four-wheeled carriages,

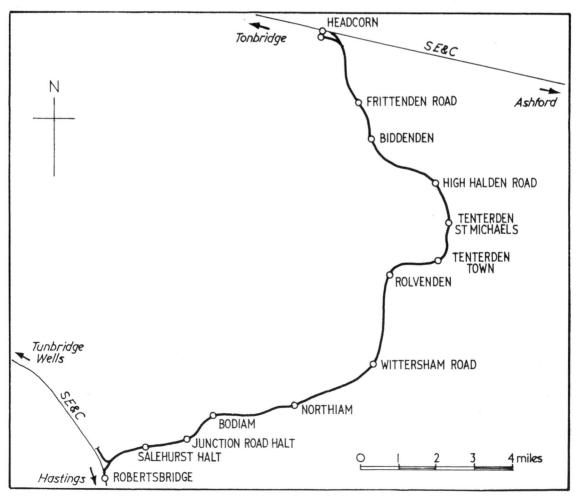

which were later in 1906 rebuilt into four bogie vehicles. Of the original four-wheeled vehicles Nos 1-4 were all thirds seating 32 passengers each; Nos 5-6 were outwardly very similar to the all thirds, but seated 28 first class passengers, with separate compartments for passengers wishing to smoke.

The Company purchased a small fleet of goods vehicles, which included two dual purpose brake vans and a selection of four-wheeled open wagons numbered 1-10. Later the Company sold most of the original goods rolling stock to the Shropshire & Montgomeryshire and the East Kent railways.

The stations along the line were built of corrugated iron with wooden framing; each station had a station master's office which was also used as a booking office, and a general waiting room. The stations had only gentlemen's outside lavatories and no running water; as if to compensate the stations always seemed to have beautiful gardens with all manner of flowers neatly kept and cared for. The stations at Northiam and Bodiam had loops with a second platform, but in the latter case the loop was later removed.

The line was extended up a 1 in 50 incline to Tenterden Town in 1903, and opened to traffic on 15 April of that year. Tenterden Town station was very different in construction from the other stations on the line, in that it was built of brick; it also had a sizeable general office, from which the line manager could control operations. The general office also had a ticket window at one end where the booking staff worked; the building had at the far end a waiting room and lamp-shed but like the other stations it also only had a gentlemen's lavatory.

On 5 May 1905 the railway was extended to Headcorn on the South Eastern Railway main line from Tonbridge to Ashford. At this time the railway changed its name to the Kent & East Sussex Railway. During this period there were plans for further extensions of the line, the main scheme being to continue from Headcorn to Maidstone, through Sutton Valence. The Maidstone line would have had a very steep incline to the north of Headcorn, where it would have ascended towards the North Downs at Sutton Valence. A number of other more local extensions were planned including lines to Pevensey, Appledore, Cranbrook and Rye, all of which were surveyed but never built.

At this time the Colonel purchased the big Hawthorn 0-8-0T *Hecate* for possible use along the main line from Headcorn to Tonbridge if agreement could be reached with SE&CR. After the Colonel's death in October 1931, Austen wasted no time in exchanging *Hecate* with the Southern Railway for a more useful locomotive, and the bogie carriages were later sold; two went to the Woolmer Instructional Military Railway (later the Longmoor Military Railway) and the third was transferred to the East Kent Railway.

The extension to Headcorn from Tenterden had been built to the standards of the South Eastern Railway, quite unlike the earlier Rother Valley Section. In later years the line was worked in two halves, because of the difference in weight restrictions on the two halves of the railway. The buildings on the Headcorn section were of wood, but similar in appearance to the buildings on the Rother Valley section.

The railway held its own through the first world war and into the 1920s, but it was during this time that the rot began to set in. After the war a vast number of motor lorry chassis became available as Government surplus and these were purchased by quite a few people returning from the war, who went straight into the road haulage business, individually in direct competition with the existing railways. It was bad enough for the main line companies but for lines like the Kent & East Sussex Railway it was almost certain death. The Company managed to make a profit for the first few years of the 1920s, but then began the slide which led to the depression, where the line was handed over to a receiver.

The railway by this time possessed a motley collection of old second-hand ex-main line vehicles. Motive power consisted of nine steam locomotives and one defunct steam railcar, plus three petrol railbus sets, two of which were Fords and one a Shefflex set. These vehicles were conventional Ford road buses on flanged wheels and coupled back-to-back. The conversions for the railbuses were carried out by Edmonds of Thetford. The railbuses drove traffic away rather than encouraging it and the management in Tonbridge was quick to be rid of them soon after the Colonel died.

It was during the mid-1930s that the Company started to hire motive power from the Southern Railway. The locomotives used by the Company were the Southern classes O1 0-6-0, A1X 0-6-0T and P 0-6-0T, although when O1s were not available the SR often sent a Class 0395 0-6-0.

The Company's own motive power was in a desperate situation by this time; of the nine locomotives only three were in working order, the remainder were standing in the dump siding at Rolvenden awaiting their fate.

The carriages were not in a very healthy state either; of the original fleet none of Hurst Nelson vehicles had survived and the Pickering steam railcar, which was used only up to 1912, was thereafter abandoned in a grass grown siding along with a number of vehicles from the North London and London & South Western railways.

However, things were changing at Tonbridge and Mr Austen had started to clear the useless worn-out rolling stock from most of the lines formerly operated by the Colonel; but before the clearance reached the Kent & East Sussex line, an event occurred which should be mentioned— the making of the film *Oh, Mr Porter* with Will Hay and his team. Locomotive No 2 *Northiam*, was patched up and sent via the Southern Railway to Basingstoke for use by the film company on the former Basingstoke & Alton Light Railway. The locomotive was fitted with a tall spiked chimney and given the name of *Gladstone* by the film company. She returned to Rolvenden in the latter part of 1937 and was withdrawn soon afterwards.

At the outbreak of war in September 1939 the KESR passed to Government control. During the first 18 months of the war the line was cleared of all derelict rolling stock and sections of track were relaid with new materials. In 1941 the Army moved in with rail-mounted guns which were stationed at Rolvenden, along with GWR Dean Goods 0-6-0 locomotives to haul them. The Army operated the rail-mounted guns between Rolvenden and Wittersham Road stations from 1941 until 1943 when they were removed. The line played a minor part in the pipeline 'Pluto' plan in connection with the D-Day invasion of occupied France. After the end of the war in 1945 the railway reverted briefly to the Tonbridge management. By this time, however, the writing was firmly on the wall for nearly all the railways in Britain, the Labour Government having pledged in its 1945 manifesto to nationalise the railways along with various other industries.

Mr Austen was not put off by this prospect though, for during the last two years leading to nationalisation the line in many ways was transformed from a run-down affair surviving by hope and charity, to a line which although not financially solvent at least looked a commercial venture.

Above right:
Locomotive No 1 *Tenterden* built by Hawthorn Leslie of Newcastle and train of four-wheelers at Rolvenden Yard in 1900, shortly before the opening of the line. Note the four-wheeled brake van for dual passenger and goods train working. At this time Rolvenden Station was known as Tenterden. Later in 1903, the line was extended up the bank to Tenterden Town, and the lower station became Rolvenden. In the background is the early locomotive shed with locomotive No 2 *Northiam* inside. Later a new brick-and-corrugated iron shed was built to replace the early timber structure.
W. H. Austen collection

Below:
Kent & East Sussex Railway 2-4-0T No 2 *Northiam*, which in the last year or so of its life was immortalised in the classic Will Hay film *Oh, Mr Porter*, for which purpose it was renamed *Gladstone*.   *L&GRP*

Station buildings were smartened up and repainted and in some cases stations were fitted for the first time with electric light, track was relaid with bullhead rail to replace flat bottom rail laid many years before, and concrete fence posts were put in along most of the line from Headcorn to Robertsbridge.

On 1 January 1948 the line passed into the hands of the British Transport Commission which at first made certain improvements to the line, mainly in permanent way. One of the schemes put forward by the new management at Waterloo was to double the track right through from Headcorn to Robertsbridge and to upgrade the track and bridges to allow U and U1 2-6-0 tender locomotives to operate through goods trains along the line.

The plan was dropped as were several other schemes to enlarge goods yards and improve the coal handling facilities. During the second world war locomotive No 3 had been rebuilt. It was in fact the last Terrier rebuilt from A1 to A1X (which involved fitting a later type Marsh boiler with extended smokebox) carried out at St Leonards Depot in 1943. In 1947 it had been sent away to Brighton for a light overhaul and repaint and when it returned to Rolvenden in early 1948 it was resplendent in Bulleid Malachite Green, with the company's initials in an arc over the number on the side tanks.

The locomotive bore its attractive livery for a short time before it was re-painted in plain, unlined British Railways black. The other surviving locomotive 0-6-0ST No 4 had been towed away, along with a collection of rotting carriages and goods vehicles, to Ashford.

During 1949-50 the Southern Region erected new mile posts along the line showing the mileage from Charing Cross. Existing ticket stocks were withdrawn and replaced with the standard British Transport Commission Edmondson card tickets. The line was now operated in two halves, from Headcorn to Tenterden Town and Tenterden Town to Robertsbridge.

The Headcorn section was operated using former SE&CR O1 0-6-0s hauling one brake carriage, normally an SE&CR Birdcage or LSWR corridor brake third, with the occasional train of goods wagons tagged on behind. The Rother Valley section was operated using LBSC A1X class 0-6-0Ts and similar coaches.

By 1953 the line was making a considerable loss and the management at Waterloo decided to close the line to passenger traffic, and keep only the original section from Robertsbridge to Tenterden Town open to goods traffic. The line closed to passenger traffic from 4 January 1954, the last train running on the previous Saturday 2 January. Lifting commenced on the Headcorn extension in mid-1955, and by the winter of that year only the trackless stations and ballast bed remained to show where the line had been.

The remaining goods trains were operated by A1X 0-6-0Ts from St Leonards depot. Operations took the form of one return trip a day, Mondays to Fridays. In 1957 the Southern Region started to use class 03 diesel-mechanical shunters on the line.

In 1958 the Locomotive Club of Great Britain chartered a train over the line from Robertsbridge to Tenterden Town, the first passenger train to Tenterden since closure in 1954, although hop-pickers' trains ran from London to Bodiam and Northiam during the hop-picking season. They were operated using non-corridor birdcage sets and A1Xs. In 1961 came the final closure to all traffic. The LCGB chartered another special train over the line on 12 July 1961; the following day saw the last goods train.

Later in 1961 a preservation society was formed to preserve the line. After a number of setbacks, which included a long legal battle in the high court, the railway was re-opened to traffic on 3 February 1974. The Tenterden Railway Company, the operating authority, is now establishing a Colonel Stephens museum in Tenterden, where it is hoped to exhibit relics from former Colonel Stephens railways.

Arrival at Tenterden in 1939 headed by Southern P Class 0-6-0T and former LSWR bogie brake third bound for Headcorn Junction. By the mid 1930s the K&ESR found that it was short of motive power and therefore had to hire locomotives from the Southern. Among them Brighton A1Xs, SECR Ps, and O1 0-6-0s, and ex-LSWR 0334 0-6-0s made an occasional appearance in the late 1940s. Note the three-arm signal, which controlled both the platforms into the loop and the track to Rolvenden. *Ken Nunn LCGB*

A train at Wittersham Road in 1953, headed by locomotive No 3 *Bodiam*, seen here as BR 32670. Wittersham Road's building was set at right angles to the platform, quite unlike the buildings on the rest of the line. *J. J. Davies collection*

Tenterden Town Station about 1910, showing No 5 *Rolvenden* and train of Pickering bogie stock about to depart for Robertsbridge Junction. At this time Tenterden had three platforms, one main, with buildings, and an island with a bay which can be seen in the photograph. Later the back bay was used for cattle traffic. The island was abandoned in early BR days leaving only the platform with the building in use. Unlike the other KESR stations Tenterden had a brick building.

W. H. Austen collection TRC

A rural scene, indeed, as O1 0-6-0 No 31065 heads a train of a single LSWR bogie brake third towards Headcorn Junction in August 1953, only four months before the Headcorn line closed in 1954. In BR days the O1s and A1Xs were the mainstay of the locomotive fleet on the line, the O1s working the Headcorn Junction-Tenterden section, and the A1Xs from Tenterden to Robertsbridge.

E. C. Griffith

Left:
One of the two former LSWR 0-6-0s owned by the Kent & East Sussex; here No 7 *Rother*, bound for Robertsbridge, pauses at Northiam with an afternoon train composed of GE four-wheel coaches.   *L&GRP*

Bottom left:
Tenterden Town station in the 1920s, with one of the Ford railbus sets standing at the platform.   *L&GRP*

Below:
Shunting outside Headcorn Junction in 1912. Rother Valley ex-LSWR No 0349 was purchased by the company in 1910 and continued in service until about 1935 when she was laid aside at Rolvenden. In 1914 *Juno*, a sister locomotive, was purchased from the LSWR as No 0284. She was also withdrawn at about the same time as *Rother.* Note the water tower and wind pump to draw up water when required, also the train make-up with a number of empty ex-SER tarpaulin wagons from the main line being made up into a train for their return. The locomotive name was painted on the centre splasher but later a cast plate was fitted.
Ken Nunn LCGB

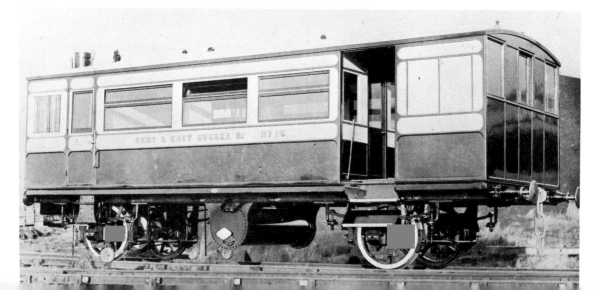

Left:
A Rother Valley Railway Hurst Nelson four-wheel coach in ex-works condition at Rolvenden yard, then called Tenterden, in 1900. The Rother Valley originally had six of these vehicles, later rebuilt by Pickering into bogie vehicles. Note the ornate lettering on the carriage side and the half-tree-trunk sleepers in the background. The Company owned two first and four third class carriages at this time. *W. H. Austen collection*

Right, and right lower:
Two types of point indicator used on the Kent & East Sussex. *L&GRP*

Left:
One of the two former LSWR royal saloons of 1848 at Rolvenden in 1930. After originally being sold by the LSWR this vehicle, along with its sister, ran on the PD&SWJR until the Colonel purchased them in 1905 for use by him as inspection vehicles. However this carriage was occasionally used on ordinary trains as it was for a time the only vehicle on the line with lights for night operation. In 1936 the saloon was purchased by the Southern Railway which intended at that time to set up a railway museum at Eastleigh. After being sent to Ashford for storage, it was later sold as a body to a farm in Kent where it perished in the early 1960s. The second vehicle finished up on the Longmoor Military Railway (see page 42). *H. C. Casserley*

(see page 42)

Left:
The Pickering steam railcar of 1905 which is reputed to have worked on the line until 1912, after which it was withdrawn and left to rot until shortly before the outbreak of world war two. The machine had an upright boiler. The chassis is more like a long wheelbase wagon underframe with extra fittings, than an underframe for a steam railcar.

This vehicle was No 16 in the carriage list and later No 6 in the locomotive list. Its underframe still exists as part of the superstructure of Rolvenden water tower. *J. S. Morgan collection*

Locomotive No 2 *Northiam* in Rolvenden shed, August 1933, showing much of the shed interior. Behind No 2 is Terrier tank No 5 *Rolvenden* undergoing a heavy general overhaul. On the right is a pile of fire bricks, and on the floor numerous hoses and bars. This photograph shows the wooden frame construction of the building very well. *H. C. Casserley*

Kent & East Sussex class A1X 0-6-0T No 3 newly repainted in Malachite Green after the second world war, and seen here with a train in 1947. *L&GRP*

Locomotives Nos 4 and 8 at Rolvenden Shed in 1935. Both had interesting careers before coming to the Kent & East Sussex Railway. No 4 originally belonged to the LSWR as No 0335. In 1932 it was exchanged by the SR along with two spare boilers in return for *Hecate* the 0-8-0T. It remained in active service until 1948 when she was withdrawn for scrap by BR. No 8 originally belonged to the North Pembroke & Fishguard Railway where she was named *Ringing Rock*, GWR No 1380. Later, on the K&ESR, its name changed to *Hesperus*. It was sold by the GWR to the line in 1914 and withdrawn in 1941. *H. C. Casserley*

An accident outside Tenterden Town Station in the late 1900s showing 'Ilfracombe goods' 0-6-0 No 7 *Rother* before naming, and a rake of GER four-wheelers. The train was bound for Robertsbridge when the rails spread. Jacks and packing gear can be seen in the foreground. The locomotive and stock were soon righted and returned to service.
W. H. Austen collection TRC

On the heap at Rolvenden in the late 1930s, locomotives *Rother* near left, *Juno* centre, and Terrier *Rolvenden*. At the same time on the other side of the wooden shed, centre of picture, there were a number of ex-NLR and LSWR carriages plus the Shefflex railbus set and the steam railcar. All the junk had been cleared by 1941 when steel prices went up considerably. No 5 was later used to rebuild No 3 *Bodiam* in the late 1930s.
H. C. Casserley

4 THE HUNDRED OF MANHOOD & SELSEY TRAMWAY
(Later the West Sussex Light Railway)

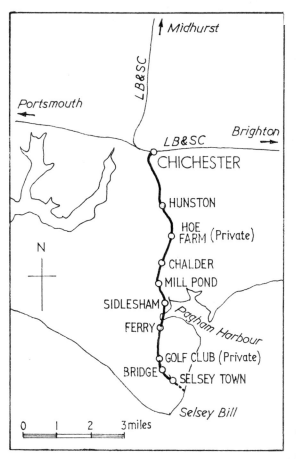

The Hundred of Manhood & Selsey Tramway opened to traffic on 27 August 1897. It ran from Chichester on the LBSCR's Portsmouth-Brighton line, via Pagham Harbour to Selsey. The Tramway was built on private land without a formal parliamentary order, and it was a number of years before any measure of legality was sought.

The Tramway served both local residents and visitors to the area at a time when there was little or no alternative transport. Apart from the tourists the Tramway also served the fishermen of Selsey and farmers along the route to Chichester. Later, after the first world war,

things changed dramatically and with the coming of the motor bus the line lost most of its revenue.

Like most of his lines Colonel Stephens proposed several schemes to extend the Selsey Tramway. In 1913 the Colonel, who was engineer of the line, proposed an extension from Hunston to Birdham, from where two branches would be built, one to East Wittering and the other to West Itchenor. The new line was surveyed in 1913 and powers were granted for its construction, but the outbreak of war in August 1914 stopped the project and it was not resumed.

The buildings along the line were constructed of corrugated iron, but unlike most of the other lines operated by the Colonel, they were smaller, normally one room affairs. Not all stations had buildings and some had only small shelters.

The Company had a strange collection of locomotives and rolling stock, mostly second and third hand. Like so many other Colonel Stephens' lines the Selsey had started with some new rolling stock, consisting of a 2-4-2T built by Peckett of Bristol in 1897, works number 681 and named *Selsey*. This, together with a rake of Falcon bogie carriages, represented the only new rolling stock the Company owned for some years.

During the Tramway's construction, the contractor had used a rather ancient saddle tank locomotive, built by Longbottom Railway Foundry in 1847 for the GWR. This locomotive was later purchased by the Tramway Company and named *Chichester*, after being rebuilt as an 0-4-2ST.

Most of the other locomotives were Manning Wardle saddle tanks purchased from contractors, although there were two exceptions, *Hesperus* from the PDSWJR, and the second *Chichester*, a Hudswell Clark engine which came from Naylor Bros, later the contractors for the Wembley Exhibition. One of the Manning Wardle tanks purchased, *Morous*, came to the line via the Stratford on Avon & Midland

Junction and the Shropshire & Montgomeryshire Railway.

During the early 1920s the Colonel introduced his petrol railbuses to the line, the first of which was the prototype of all his railbuses—the Wolseley Sidley vehicle, built on a chassis purchased after the first world war, with a body built in Maidstone. The Wolseley Sidley was used for trials on the line, and later put into normal service.

The railcar was operated on the line coupled to a Ford road lorry, but occasionally the unit was turned. This was done at Chichester, on the Southern turntable. One morning the car was being turned when the rear portion of the vehicle, which like the front unit, had a radiator, struck a steel post by the side of the turntable and was damaged beyond repair. As it was not a great success the unit was withdrawn. The railcar was later taken to Kinnerley on the S&M where the body was used to refurbish the former LCC tramcar for *Gazelle*.

Not long after the accident the Ford set arrived in 1923. Later, in 1928, this was joined by a Shefflex set. The railcars often trailed a luggage trolley behind them on their journey from Selsey to Chichester and occasionally the trolleys were used by the permanent way department for track ballast. The other carriage stock consisted of former Lambourn Valley and LC&DR vehicles. The Company also had a small fleet of open wagons and vans. One of the former Rother Valley brake vans was used on the line.

The Tramway had an uneventful career through the first world war, but during the 1920s things began to liven up for a time. On

The first locomotive, named *Chichester,* also the contractor's locomotive for the line, is seen here being towed along the road near Hunston in 1897 before the line was opened. The need for this feat arose when the locomotive was needed on the lower section, but was at work on the upper part. This was before the canal bridge was built and the only way was to haul the engine along the road behind the traction engine. Temporary rails were laid in front of the engine and taken up behind. The locomotive, an 0-6-0ST, has had its rear coupling rods removed and is technically running as an 0-4-2ST. After the line opened in August 1897 it was properly rebuilt as an 0-4-2ST using a small pair of trailing wheels.   *E. C. Griffith collection*

3 September 1923, there occurred the worst accident in the Tramway's history. Accidents had occurred on the Tramway over the years before this, but all previous accidents were minor compared with what happened that day.

The 8.15 a.m. tram from Selsey to Chichester, hauled by the second locomotive named *Chichester*, lurched off the track near Golf Club Halt, killing the fireman and badly injuring the driver. None of the passengers on the train were hurt though. The line was closed for two days as a result of the accident. One result was that the Colonel and his management were blamed for negligence, for it appeared that this stretch of tramway had not been relaid for many years and the sleepers were completely rotten.

In 1924 the Tramway took a step towards legality, when an order under the Railway Construction Facilities Act, was granted, which allowed a new company to be formed. This was empowered to take over the HM&ST and all its assets. From January 1924 the Company was known as the West Sussex Railway.

During the 1920s and early 1930s the

Tramway declined and no improvements were carried out. The decline mainly arose from competition by new bus services operating between Chichester and the outlying districts, and as the Tramway was noted for being very slow, people quickly changed their mode of transport when buses appeared on the scene.

In 1924 the Company's finances were in such a mess that the concern could not afford to pay its debentures and several writs were taken out against it. It was after a number of cases had been heard that the high court placed a receiver in charge of matters and the end was in sight. Several offers were made for the line, one from Sir Herbert Walker, General Manager of the Southern Railway, who wished to reconstruct the line as an extension of his electrified system. An alternative offer was made by Henry Greenly, who at the time was looking for a suitable location for a miniature railway for Captain Howey. Later a more convenient site was found for him on the Kent coast between New Romney and Hythe.

By 1934 it was obvious that the Tramway had but a little time to go, a number of the locomotives were out of use and both passenger and goods rolling stock was in a deplorable state. Worst of all, the permanent way was so badly worn in places that the original contractors' rail had been reduced from 41 lb/yd to 25 lb/yd. On 19 January 1935, notices were posted, informing the travelling public that the Tramway was at last closing. It was on that evening that the last train ran from Selsey to Chichester.

The Tramway operated for a week after passenger closures, to clear goods traffic and bring items of rolling stock up from Selsey shed in readiness for the forthcoming sale.

No official order was made by the Ministry of Transport to abandon the line. At the sale that followed all the locomotives and rolling stock went for scrap. Some of the items sold were in fact the property of the Colonel himself and the money from the sale of these items went to his executors.

A number of carriage and van bodies could still be found in the Chichester area until fairly recently. The Tramway was lifted during 1936, although a number of buildings and other structures remained for a number of years after closure.

The Tramway was greatly loved by locals and enthusiasts alike, and as always, with these lines there were some amusing tales told about it. One true story involved the first *Chichester* when the Tramway was under construction. The contractors' locomotive which was at the time working on the northern part of the Tramway was needed for construction work on the southern part of the line. The lifting bridge over the canal at Hunston had not then been completed. Because of the gap the locomotive had to be towed behind a traction engine along the road to the site of Hunston Station. A gang of navvies laid rails in front and retrieved them behind, as the machine was towed along.

The Tramway also had its nickname, some called it the Tram, some the Selsey Bumper, but others at the Colonel's office in Tonbridge called it the Death Trap! In the late 1920s a local group of folk singers composed a ditty entitled the *Sidlesham Snail*. The Station Master at Chichester was so annoyed about this tune that he said he would sack any staff member that he heard whistling or singing it.

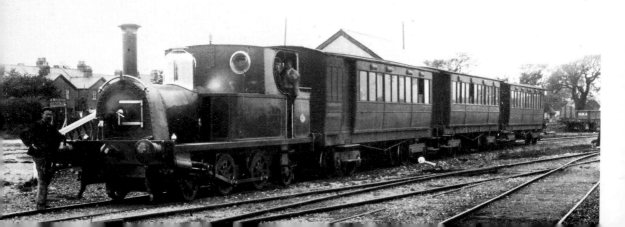

Above:
Manning Wardle saddle tank *Sidlesham*, built in 1861, crosses the canal bridge in 1900 with a train for Selsey, consisting of two Falcon carriages built new for the line in 1896. The bridge mechanism and lifting equipment are clearly seen. *E. C. Griffith collection*

Below left:
What a splendidly unusual locomotive—an outside cylinder 2-4-2T with a sparkling brass dome. This engine *Selsey* was Peckett works No 681 of 1897 and the train of Falcon bogie stock is seen at Selsey in 1900. Later, around 1899 the locomotive was rebuilt extensively with larger tanks and modified coal bunker. It was withdrawn for scrap when the tramway closed in 1935 and cut up in 1936. *Lens of Sutton*

Below:
Jacking and packing the second *Chichester* after a minor accident near Chalder in the late 1920s. In this case the platelayer responsible was found to be at fault for not doing his job properly and was duly dismissed. The locomotive depicted originally belonged to the East Cornwall Mineral Railway, a 3ft 6in gauge mineral line, part of which was taken over by the PD&SWJR in 1908. The locomotive was converted from narrow to standard gauge for use as a shunting locomotive at Callington. It was sold from the PD&SWJR in 1919 and withdrawn in 1932. *E. C. Griffith collection*

Locomotives *Sidlesham* and *Chichester* at Selsey shed in 1898. *Chichester*, a former contractor's locomotive, was extensively rebuilt, and in this photograph is seen painted black, while *Sidlesham* is painted in an ornate lined green livery. *Chichester* was built as an 0-6-0ST by the Long Bottom Railway Foundry in 1847 for the GWR. Later the locomotive was sold to Peckett of Bristol, and in turn it came to the Selsey tramway in 1897.

E. C. Griffith collection

Manning Wardle saddle tank *Morous* in Selsey shed in the late 1920s, showing extensive repairs in progress. *Morous* was originally a contractor's locomotive and worked for the Stratford-on-Avon & Midland Junction Railway before going to the Shropshire & Montgomeryshire Railway in 1910. It was later transferred to the Selsey tramway in 1924 after a number of years out of use and was cut up on site at Chichester in 1936.

Ken Nunn LCGB

The great flood of 1910: *Sidlesham* and ex-GER open wagons are here seen at Sidlesham during the local disaster while repairs were in hand. Train services ceased and a horse bus operated the service.

E. C. Griffith

Above:
Chalder Station in 1900, only a few years after the tramway opened. The buildings along the line were of very similar construction to each other; the station building is built of corrugated iron with its awning having v-shaped upper supports; the platform was faced in concrete and Midland fencing was used. The station nameboard has contractor's lettering style.

E. C. Griffith collection

Top:
A Ford railbus set at Chichester in 1927, showing the station buildings and gas holders in background. The site is now still used to store oil tank wagons from the Southern Region.

Lens of Sutton

Below:
Derelict coaches of the West Sussex Railway standing at Selsey after closure in 1935.

C. R. L. Coles

5 THE SHROPSHIRE & MONTGOMERYSHIRE RAILWAY

The story of the Shropshire & Montgomeryshire Railway was long and complicated. It started life in 1866 as the Potteries, Shrewsbury and North Wales Railway. 'The Potts', as it was locally called, was not a great success and through financial troubles the line closed to traffic in 1880. The original company had constructed only the middle section of the line from Shrewsbury to Blodwell Junction, near Nantmawr Quarry. There were a number of moves to reopen the line made locally in the years after the first closure. Several schemes were put forward over the first 20 years of closure, the most notable of which was the Shropshire Railway Company, which was formed partly by the Potteries shareholders, in a last ditch attempt to retrieve some of their lost money.

The Shropshire Railway Company, formed in the early 1890s, went about raising money to rebuild and reopen the line, but it, like so many schemes of its kind, fell by the wayside and the railway was left to slumber on again until the early years of the 20th century, when the Colonel and the Light Railways Act were to change the situation.

During the period of closure from 1880 until 1910 when the line reopened as the Shropshire and Montgomeryshire Railway, a Mr Reeves looked after the line on behalf of the receiver.

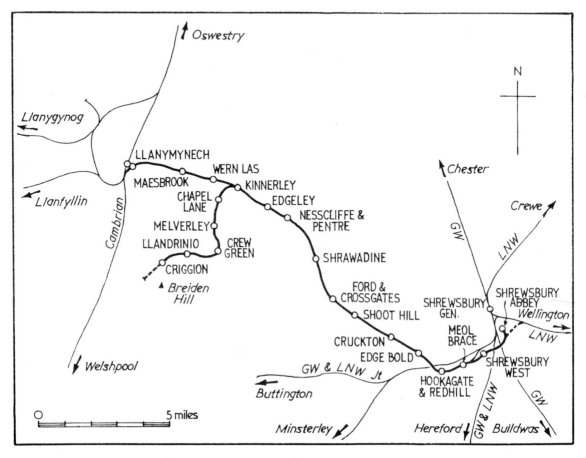

Shrewsbury Abbey Station in about 1870, during the regime of the Potteries, Shrewsbury & North Wales Railway, with an LNWR 0-4-2 and four-wheeled stock.
L&GRP

Mr Reeves had been the guard on the last train of the old Potts and was among the people who travelled on the first train in 1910, when his words to Colonel Stephens were 'now I can die a happy man'.

Guard Reeves patrolled the line with the aid of a plate-layers pump trolley, making sure the fences and permanent way stayed in reasonable order. The receiver had kept a skeleton staff at Shrewsbury and Llanymynech to look after the locomotives and rolling stock, most of which was sold in an auction held at Shrewsbury Abbey Foregate in 1888. The rolling stock which remained, mostly wagons, were left to rot at various locations up and down the line.

During the mid-1900s there was a revival of interest in the campaign to reopen the line, but this time the voices of the local people did not fall on deaf ears, for other people outside the district including the Colonel were also interested. In late 1909 the Colonel had the railway surveyed and new plans were drawn up to reopen it as a light railway. During 1910 contractors moved in and transformed the railway, entangled with weeds and shrubs, with newly relaid track and newly rebuilt buildings; however many of the original buildings built by the old Potteries Railway were renovated and reused for the purpose for which they were built.

During the rebuilding many of the original track components, particularly cast chairs and rails, were torn from their rotten sleepers and used again.

The railway was reopened to traffic on 13 April 1911 amid much public rejoicing in villages along the route of the line, as *Hesperus*, the former LSWR 'Ilfracombe goods' and its train of ex-Midland non-corridor stock, rolled along the line from Shrewsbury Abbey Station to Llanymynech.

The locomotives and rolling stock were maintained at a new shed and workshop built at Kinnerley at the junction of the branch to Criggion; these buildings were adequate not only for light repairs but also for the heaviest of the overhauls required to keep locomotives and stock running on the line. The branch to Criggion was reopened to traffic a year after the main line, in the summer of 1912. It served a quarry at Criggion which was worked by the BQC quarry company.

Although the railway had been easy enough to renovate and reopen, there had been some snags when it came to bridges and the two viaducts along the line. At Shrawardine, on the main line, the structure had to be strengthened and replated, but the wooden trestle at Melverley needed complete rebuilding, the original having collapsed in 1902.

Not all of the former Potteries line was reopened by the Colonel; the Cambrian had purchased the section of line from Llanymynech to Blodwell Junction in 1912 in connection with its Tanat Valley project.

The Colonel purchased a strange variety of stock for the S&M. Locomotive No 1 was the famous diminutive well tank *Gazelle* built by Dodman of Kings Lynn in 1893 for the Mayor of the town. The machine was originally a 2-2-2WT but after its arrival on the Shropshire & Montgomeryshire it was rebuilt as an 0-4-2WT, in order to work with the converted ex-LCC tramcar on the Criggion branch.

As on other lines operated by the Colonel, he also purchased some new locomotives, in this case two 0-6-2Ts from Hawthorn Leslie of Newcastle. The machines were named *Pyramus*, works No 2878 of 1911 and *Thisbe*, works No 2879 also of 1911. After a short time both locomotives were resold to the military authorities, who after the first world war disposed of *Pyramus* to a colliery while retaining *Thisbe* until the late 1930s for use on the Longmoor Military Railway.

Being concerned to provide more motive power than really needed the Colonel overstocked the locomotive shed, in this case with three Terriers, two LSWR 'Ilfracombe goods' 0-6-0s and lastly the most incredible locomotive of all excluding *Gazelle*, a former Bury 0-4-0 originally built for the Shrewsbury & Hereford Railway in 1840. Later rebuilt as an 0-4-2ST, after sale to the Griff Colliery Company in the 1860s, the engine, originally named *Hecate*, and later renamed *Severn*, arrived on the line in 1911 and despite its great age operated trains until the late 1920s.

When most of the steam fleet needed renewal in the late 1920s the Company purchased three LNWR 0-6-0 tender locomotives. The railway had a three-car Ford railbus set and a Ford lorry, which was often coupled to a Ford trailer when working the line.

The Wolseley Sidley car which was used on the Selsey line was stored at Kinnerley for many years, but following its accident on the Selsey line, the machine was never run on the S&M. Austen presumably sent it to Kinnerley from Selsey to use the body for conversion on to the LCC tramcar chassis actually carried out in the late 1930s. The railway lost its passenger service on 6 November 1933; however, parties could still hire a train if they wished and there are many stories of *Gazelle* and its newly refurbished trailer car being used to take people on excursions up the line long after regular passenger trains had gone.

The passenger stock in its day had consisted of a set of four bogie Midland vehicles, several four-wheeled carriages of Midland, North Staffordshire and London & South Western origin, plus one odd Great Eastern vehicle.

An ex-LNWR 0-6-0 heads a train on an outward journey from Llanymynech to Kinnerley in 1931. The train consists of the ex-LSWR royal saloon of 1844 and two ex-Midland bogie non-corridor third class vehicles. Three former LNWR 0-6-0s were purchased for the S&M, LMS Nos 8108, 8182, 8236. In 1939 No 8108 was repainted in Southern Railway olive green and lined. After the War Department took over, the locomotive reverted to black and was given back its old number.
Lens of Sutton

Like the K&ESR, the S&M also had an LSWR Royal carriage of the 1840s, which was later taken to Longmoor. This was used by the Colonel during his yearly inspection of the line.

The goods stock consisted of a variety of Midland, LSWR and NSR wagons. The line carried on through the bad years of the mid-1930s until the outbreak of war in September 1939 when it came under military control. Commercial traffic until then was still being managed from Tonbridge. However, before 1939, Austen had cleared all the derelict rolling stock from Kinnerley yard, which made the line look quite uncommonly neat and tidy.

Shortly after the outbreak of war in 1939, the Army took over and used a number of stations along the route as supply dumps, and continued to do so until 1960 when the line was closed. However, the Criggion branch was not taken over, and trains of stone from the BQC Quarry had to be specially arranged in the Army timetable. For this reason the line had a civilian line controller from the end of the second world war until 1960.

During the years of military operation, the line saw several new types of locomotives and stock, including Austerity 0-6-0STs and GWR Dean goods locomotives, and a set of former LT&SR bogie carriages which were used on the railway to transport Army Staff from one supply dump to the next. These particular coaches were notable since they had corridors and had been built for the Ealing-Southend through service. The final closure came on 29 February 1960, when the last train ran from Llanymynech to Shrewsbury Abbey Station, after which the Army handed over the line to the Western Region for demolition.

Approaching Kinnerley from Llanymynech in 1930 is a double-header consisting of *Pyramus*, an ex-LSWR 'Ilfracombe Goods' 0-6-0, and *Dido* an ex-LBSCR Terrier. The stock again includes Midland four-wheeled full brake and two four-wheel former LSWR coaches. The S&M had three former Brighton A1 Terrier 0-6-0Ts, named *Dido*, *Daphne* and *Hecate*. Unlike other lines run by the Colonel, the Terriers on the S&M were not a great success; this is one of the few photographs showing a Terrier at work on this line.

Real Photographs

Passengers waiting at Shrewsbury Abbey Station in the late 1920s with an LNWR DX 0-6-0 on loan from Shrewsbury LMS shed and a train of ex-Midland stock. In the background are the two water towers that then served the station. The platform water tower is now in the hands of the Tenterden Railway Co, which has taken over part of the Kent & East Sussex as a tourist line, and will be re-erected in the future.

W. H. Austen collection TRC

Kinnerley Junction shed, water tower and approach lines, photographed in September 1938. *L&GRP*

Former LSWR 0-6-0 *Hesperus* at Shrewsbury Abbey Station in late 1937, awaiting the road to Kinnerley with the morning parcels train. Dirty, rusty and leaking steam like a sieve, in this condition the old South Western engine ran for another three years until finally withdrawn under Army control in 1940. *Lens of Sutton*

Kinnerley locomotive shed in the late 1920s showing an 'Ilfracombe goods' 0-6-0 under repair and 0-4-2ST No 2 *Severn* in store. *Severn* had an interesting history; it started life as an 0-4-0 in 1840 on the Shrewsbury & Hereford Railway. Later it was purchased by the Griff Colliery Co and rebuilt as an 0-4-2T in 1911, when it was bought by the Colonel and renamed *Hecate*. Later it reverted to the name *Severn* and was withdrawn in the early 1930s. Note the belt machinery on the far left used for repairing locomotives and stock.

W. H. Austen collection TRC

Gazelle and the Wolseley Sidley trailer at Criggion in 1939 with a Birmingham Locomotive Club special. By this time the locomotive had acquired a coat of Southern olive green with white lining. The locomotive and saloon were used for inspection work, although it was possible to hire both for excursions up the line on weekends. Later during the second world war the locomotive was detached from the saloon and ran as a track testing unit, to sniff out obstacles and mines that might have been laid during the night. After the war both Gazelle and the old LSWR royal saloon were sent to Longmoor in Hampshire where it was hoped to preserve them. However the royal saloon was so full of woodworm that it was broken up and burnt. Gazelle happily survived to be put at first on a length of track at Longmoor army camp and more recently was sent to York Railway Museum where it can be seen in Longmoor blue livery. *Lens of Sutton*

Kinnerley locomotive shed in 1911, shortly after completion, showing the Dodman 2-2-2WT Gazelle just delivered from T. W. Ward of Sheffield. The locomotive was originally the property of the Mayor of Kings Lynn who was a locomotive enthusiast of the last century. Built by Dodman of Kings Lynn in 1893 to a private order she once journeyed from Kings Lynn to York over the GER and GNR lines. Later after the death of her owner she was sold to T. W. Ward of Sheffield, from whom the Colonel purchased her in 1910 for use as an inspection locomotive. *LPC Ian Allan*

A very derelict-looking 0-4-2 Gazelle in 1935. Fortunately it survived and has been preserved at the National Railway Museum, York. *L&GRP*

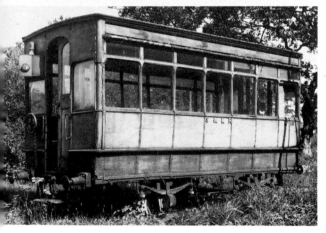

Above:
One of the Midland Railway bogie coaches bought by the Shropshire & Montgomeryshire Railway, seen here soon after arrival. *L&GRP*

Left upper:
One of the pair of former LSW Royal saloons of the 1840s which Colonel Stephens used on two of his lines; this is the one on the Shropshire & Montgomeryshire Railway seen after withdrawal and should be compared with the companion vehicle on the Kent & East Sussex, illustrated on page 26. The S&M vehicle eventually found its way to the Longmoor Military Railway where it was hoped to restore it for preservation but it was found that the bodywork had rotted too badly or been eaten away. *L&GRP*

Left lower:
The former LCC horse tram carriage, here seen dumped at Kinnerley yard in 1935. *Gazelle* was rebuilt from a 2-2-2WT to an 0-4-2WT shortly after its arrival in 1911. The tramcar and the locomotive were paired up to form a makeshift auto-train to operate the Criggion branch passenger service. Later after the closure of the line to passenger traffic the body of the wooden tramcar was removed and replaced with the body of the Wolseley Sidley railcar which had by that time arrived from the Selsey tramway. *Lens of Sutton*

Below:
Kinnerley Junction Station, with a line of passenger coaches photographed in September 1938, five years after passenger services were withdrawn. Nearest the camera are two of the former Midland bogie coaches and fourth from the near end is the former LSWR Royal saloon. *L&GRP*

Shrawardine Station on the Shropshire & Montgomery-shire Railway, with its raised platform and neat timber building. Note the diamond-shaped signal on the platform, face-on to the driver when at danger and edge-on when clear. *L&GRP*

Llanymynech Station showing the western end of the S&M coming in from the left to join the Cambrian line from Oswestry to Welshpool. *L&GRP*

and brick structures at main stations. At halts small neat wooden shelters were built. The locomotive depot and workshop was situated at Clevedon, although rolling stock was sometimes repaired at Portishead.

The railway mostly served the tourists in the area although, in the off-peak season, local goods and farm produce predominated. The line held its own through the 1920s and early 1930s but by 1936 the railway began to feel the pinch from the motor bus operators and the depression. The Colonel had operated a small fleet of coastal craft in the 1920s and most of this fleet, which transported goods from the South Wales coast to Wick St Lawrence Quay, was sold by the mid-1930s leaving a gap in the railway's economy.

The Colonel tried several experiments in an attempt to ease the cost of running and maintaining the line. One idea involved using individual concrete slabs under each rail instead of wooden sleepers. The slabs were held together by old point and signal rodding. The same thing was also tried on part of the Kent & East Sussex railway in early 1930s, near Headcorn. It was one of the first applications of concrete as sleepers, today used in many parts of the world.

After the Colonel died the line passed into the hands of Austen, who was appointed receiver by the shareholders. Austen managed the line through the last difficult years until the outbreak of war in September 1939 but it was at this time that the Excess Insurance Company bought out all the other shareholders and gave Austen orders to close the line from 18 May

1940. Economic circumstances finally won.

Despite the war a large number of people turned out to see the last train run between Portishead and Weston-super-Mare. However, all was not quite over because, following the invasion of France by the Germans, the South Wales ports were jammed full of coal normally exported to the French ports. The Government ordered the Great Western to take over the WC&PR together with any serviceable rolling stock and to use the railway for coal storage. The only stock worth having as far as the GWR was concerned were the two Brighton A1X Terriers No 2 *Portishead* and No 4.

After overhaul the locomotives were operated by the GWR first on the WC&PR and then at locations on the GWR, but were found to be lacking power for heavy work. They became GWR Nos 5 and 6; the latter was cut up in 1948 but No 5 survived until 1954. The rest of the rolling stock was sold and cut up in late 1940 or early 1941. WC&P saddle tank No 5, built in 1919 by Manning Wardle, was sold out of service to industry in late 1940.

The Great Western abandoned the temporary use of the line in mid-1941 and the scrap merchants moved in; by mid-1942 the railway had been lifted. Much of the old rail had originally come from the Krupp Steel Works of Essen and now it was destined to return there in a very different shape.

Today little survives of the line. Most of the buildings are no more and the track bed has largely been obliterated by building and reclamation by farmers.

Manning Wardle 0-6-0ST No 5, at Clevedon with a train of former Metropolitan four-wheelers ready to leave for Weston in 1923. This locomotive was acquired in 1919 in practically new condition. In its early days it bore the name *Hecate*. Later, before 1923, these plates were removed and it ran from then until 1940, when it was sold for industrial use, without a name. The carriages are Metropolitan. Note the Midland open wagon next to rear carriage, probably then only recently purchased for the line's internal traffic when this photograph was taken. *Ken Nunn LCGB*

Right:
One of the former LBSCR Terrier 0-6-0Ts, originally No 53 *Ashtead*, built in 1875, and sold to the Weston, Clevedon & Portishead becoming No. 4. It became GWR property in 1940 and bore the number 6 but was scrapped in 1948. *L&GRP*

A scene at Clevedon locomotive shed in 1929 showing former Jersey Railway 2-4-0T *General Don,* renamed *Clevedon,* No 1 on the WC&PR. Behind is seen ex-GWR 2-4-0T No 1384 and WC&PR No 4 *Hesperus. Clevedon* was not well liked by the locomotive crews.
Author's collection

The former GWR 2-4-0T No 1384 seen here at Weston in 1911, shortly after its acquisition. This locomotive had a very interesting background. It was built by Sharp Stewart in 1876 and first worked on the Princes Risborough & Watlington Railway, which was later acquired by the GWR. After this it became No 1384, spending most of the rest of her GWR career on various short branch lines on that company's system. In 1911 it was acquired by the WC&PR for use on passenger trains. It was withdrawn in mid-1930s and cut up in 1940, after the line's closure. *LPC Ian Allan*

Above:
A general view of Clevedon Station shed and works taken in June 1937.   *L&GRP*

Left:
Roadside halt at Broadstone consisting of nothing more than a level crossing and a hut.   *L&GRP*

Below:
The small Drewry petrol railcar of 1921, here seen at Portishead in the early 1920s. Summer passenger traffic, particularly at weekends, could be heavy at this time. The small Drewry had an unpowered trailer which was also often used with the large Drewry car. Unlike the Ford and Shefflex sets on the other lines managed by the Colonel, the Drewry cars were quite advanced in their design and were much more comfortable to travel in.   *Photomatic/H. Smith collection*

Above:
Two of the WC&P's end balcony bogie coaches purchased from the Lancaster Railway Carriage & Wagon Co after a cancelled South American order.
L&GRP

Among the WC&P's rolling stock were some old four-wheel coaches bought secondhand from other railways; *below* is a pair of LSW close-coupled four-wheel saloons and *bottom* a pair of former Metropolitan third class coaches. Notice the additional lower footboards provided to give access from low level platforms.
L&GRP

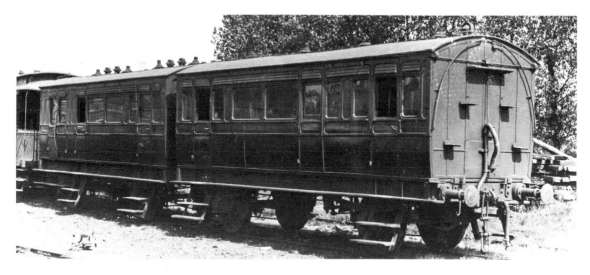

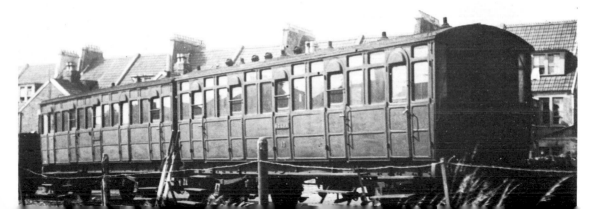

The WC&P was nothing if not modern when it came to control of level crossings, at least where it passed over the main Bristol-Weston road. Traffic lights were installed to control road traffic, triggered off when the train operated a treadle at the approaches to the crossing. (*Left*). Traffic light indications were also displayed to the approaching train with a green aspect shown when the lights for road traffic were at red.

L&GRP

Below:
Wick St Lawrence wharf near the mouth of the River Yeo, used for transferring goods from the small coastal fleet, also owned by Colonel Stephens, which plied between South Wales ports and Wick St Lawrence.

L&GRP

7 THE ASHOVER LIGHT RAILWAY

The Ashover Light Railway was the last narrow gauge line to be built by the Colonel. The line served a group of stone quarries owned by the Clay Cross Company in Derbyshire. It ran from Clay Cross on the LMS main line between Derby and Chesterfield to Ashover Butts. Along its course it served a number of stone quarries and an open-cast coal mine, near Chesterfield Road Station. The mainstay of the traffic was granite chippings used by the LMS for ballast and for which the Company had a permanent contract.

The idea of a light railway connecting the quarries was first put forward by the Clay Cross Company before the first world war, but indecision and the outbreak of war prevented anything being done until 1919 when the Jackson family, the owners of the Clay Cross Company, rekindled interest in the scheme.

It was intended from the start that the line would be a mineral line, and no thought was given to operating a passenger service; however, the Board of Trade had other intentions and the Company was slowly coaxed into the idea of a passenger service, much to the annoyance of the Jackson family.

Originally the line was to be standard gauge, but with material shortages after the war and on the advice given by Colonel Stephens, the Clay Cross management agreed to a 60cm gauge line instead, since narrow gauge materials were available having been used to provide supply railways in Europe during the conflict. The first

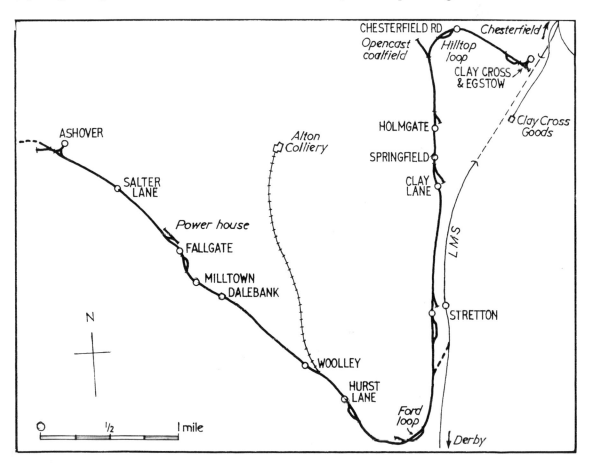

sod was cut at Fallgate on 22 December 1922 and work steadily progressed over the next two years until spring 1924 when a special train worked through from Clay Cross to Fallgate, invited guests riding in open wagons for the occasion. T. H. Jackson rode in fine style seated in his armchair.

Originally the Company purchased four Baldwin 4-6-0Ts from the War Disposals Board. These locomotives had been used by the British Army on the western front ordnance light railways of the war, together with a fleet of Hudson bogie open wagons for stone traffic. The locomotives were named after the children of General Jackson, the acting General Manager of the Clay Cross Company. Of the first four the names were *Guy*, *Hummy*, *Peggy* and *Joan*; later two more locomotives were purchased from T. W. Ward of Sheffield, also Baldwin 4-6-0Ts, one being named *Bridget* and the second being given *Guy*'s nameplates when it was found that the original locomotive bearing that name was in need of extensive repairs.

The original *Guy* was later stored at Clay Cross carriage shed until dismantled for spare parts between 1939 and 1942, when the remains were cut up for scrap.

The passenger carriages used on the railway were built by the Gloucester Railway Carriage & Wagon Company in 1924, and were numbered 1 to 4 on the Company's list. Each vehicle was vacuum braked and had a centre coupling. The carriage bodies were new, but the running gear was second hand WD Hudson bogies purchased from the War Disposals Board.

The stations along the line were built shortly after the railway had opened to mineral traffic. The buildings were quite unlike any of the buildings on the other railways operated by the Colonel. All were of wood, some having a combined office and goods store, and others having just a simple but neat shelter. At Ashover Butts a cafe was built, and named *Where the Rainbow Ends*; it was here that the staff would often while away the time between turns on the passenger service.

The railway formally opened to passenger traffic on the 6 April 1925. T. H. Jackson at the age of 91 officiated at the ceremony and travelled on the first train. Although the day went well, and for some time the little railway was very popular with the locals, the management was still not happy at having to run passenger trains.

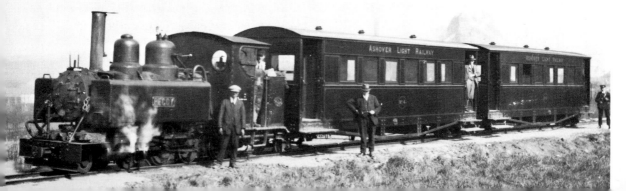

Ashover Butts' Station soon after the opening of the line in 1925. The station was located just outside the village at the bottom of a hill. The run round facilities here were in the form of a triangle, where the complete train reversed and then backed into the platform after turning. Note the building with its office on one side and goods store on the other, also in the foreground the former WD bogie open wagons lettered ALR. Like most of the stock they were purchased secondhand as war surplus by the company. *LPC Ian Allan*

In the late 1920s and early 1930s the railway played its part in transportation for the district. Not only were ordinary everyday trains run but also special Sunday and Bank Holiday excursions. Nevertheless when the passenger service started to make a loss in 1930 the management of the Clay Cross Company wasted no time in suggesting that all passenger services should be terminated and from the end of October 1931 the line ceased to operate regular passenger trains.

However, passenger trains still operated during the summer and on bank holidays until September 1936, when the carriages were stored in a siding near Ashover Butts, in case the need arose for their use again. In addition to the original bogie carriages, the Company purchased eight short-wheelbase bogie vehicles from the Wembley Exhibition when it closed in late 1925. These were the carriages which had been in use on the Exhibition's Never-stop railway and were badly needed because of the gross overcrowding owing to the popularity of the Ashover line in its first season. Later after the line closed to passenger traffic, the Never-stop vehicles were shunted into a siding and left to decay, finally being broken up in 1942. The Company also purchased one of the former Leek & Manifold transporter wagons to carry standard gauge wagons, which was not a great success after its gauge was altered from 2ft 6in to 60cm. This vehicle was broken up with other items of rolling stock in 1942.

The railway enjoyed a new lease of life during the second world war when the quarries and open-cast coal mine were very active. Often at this time a Baldwin would haul a train of full

Baldwin 4-6-0T *Peggy* and train near Chesterfield Road shortly after opening of the ALR in 1925. The locomotives and carriage stock were elaborately lined during this period, the livery being Midland Crimson Lake lined in yellow straw. The goods stock was painted in light grey with white lettering shaded black. Note the stove-pipe chimney with its rainwater flap on the Baldwin. Later the stove pipes were replaced with chimneys of a heavier cast type. *LPC Ian Allan*

stone wagons from Ashover to Chesterfield Road where it would pick up a further load of coal and continue to Clay Cross, with the stone wagons behind and the coal wagons coupled in front. During the latter part of the war the Baldwins started to wear out, and gradually one by one the locomotives were cannibalised to provide parts to keep sister machines in traffic.

The Company had purchased ten 60cm gauge Dick, Kerr petrol-electric locomotives shortly after the first world war. These machines were not used as locomotives but were used as stationary generators for a number of years.

One of the petrol locomotives, later named *Amos*, was overhauled at the Company's works at Clay Cross in 1928 and set to work shunting the yard at Clay Cross and banking stone trains up the incline at Hurst Lane. It was later rebuilt and re-gauged to run on standard gauge track. *Amos* was scrapped in 1964 after being sold out of service to a contractor.

A Muir Hill geared tractor was purchased in 1940 for use in Fallgate Yard but was rarely used; it resembled a Fordson tractor on a narrow gauge frame and was cut up in 1945. The Muir Hill was replaced by a Planet diesel locomotive which shunted Fallgate Yard for a time before being sold to George Cohen, for use on one of his contracts on Canvey Island. This was replaced with a Ransome-Rapier diesel unit which was used until the system closed completely in 1963.

After the war the stone traffic began to decline and in 1948 when the railways were nationalised the Clay Cross Company lost the contract for ballast. The railway slowly closed down between 1948 and 1950 when the line was abandoned completely although the yard at Fallgate carried on functioning, using diesel locomotives, until late 1963. All repairs to locomotives and rolling stock were carried out at the Company's workshops at Clay Cross and it was here that the remaining Baldwins and some of the open wagons were cut up in 1951.

Today little remains of the railway. The Planet diesel has been privately preserved and a number of small relics from the line are in private hands. These include some of the nameplates on display at the narrow-gauge museum at Towyn. Also two of the carriages are preserved on the Lincolnshire Coast Light Railway. *Where the Rainbow Ends* cafe was re-erected at Clay Cross Sports Ground and is still there.

In the years after the passenger service had ceased special passenger trains were still worked using open wagons fitted with seats. These trains were run for the Clay Cross Company workers on Bank Holidays and company sports days when trains were run between Clay Cross and Ashover Butts. The train is seen here at Ashover Butts during a bank holiday in 1946 with Baldwin 4-6-0T *Joan* in charge.   *Real Photographs*

An unidentified Baldwin 4-6-0T at Woolley in the heart of rural Derbyshire in 1946 with a train of stone, bound for Clay Cross LMS exchange sidings. In the latter years of the line most of the traffic from the stone quarries was for the LMS for use as permanent way ballast. This traffic ceased at nationalisation in 1948. The cancellation of this regular traffic was a major factor in the decision by the Clay Cross Company to close the line.   *I. Gotheridge collection*

A battered *Peggy* takes water at Clay Cross stone crushing plant in 1949, with a stone train for the exchange sidings. There were only two serviceable Baldwins at this time, *Peggy* and *Joan*. Although *Peggy* was the locomotive in regular use (*Joan* being an unpopular locomotive because it was rough riding), both were cut up on site at Clay Cross in 1951.

H. Skinner collection

9   THE FESTINIOG RAILWAY (For Welsh Highland Railway—see page 66)

The Festiniog Railway is one of the most famous narrow gauge railways in the world. Many articles and books have been written about this historic line but Colonel Stephens' connections date only from 1923, when he took over the locomotive superintendency and civil engineer's positions of both the Festiniog and Welsh Highland railways until his death in 1931, after which Austen and his team looked after both railways until they closed.

The Festiniog was opened as a horse tramway on 20 April 1836. It was built to the 60cm gauge and ran from Porthmadog to Blaenau Ffestiniog, where it served the local slate quarries. In 1863 the railway made history by being the first narrow-gauge line to use steam locomotives. Much of this great achievement can be put down to the Spooner family who not only engineered the Festiniog but were also responsible for the setting up of the ill-fated North Wales Narrow Gauge Railway. The story of the FR as a Stephens line really begins after the first world war. The Festiniog had enjoyed great prosperity in pre-war days, but such times did not return after the conflict was over and because of a combination of the slump in the slate industry and road competition, the company's receipts looked pretty grim in the early 1920s.

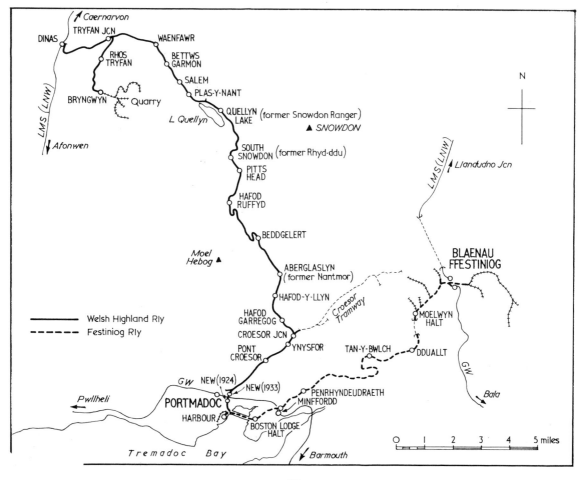

The Colonel by this time had earned himself a reputation for his ability to run unremunerative light railways, which prompted the Board of the Festiniog Railway to ask him to join the Company in a managerial capacity, in order to try and put the books straight.

It so happened that the Colonel was engaged with the Welsh Highland Light Railway in a similar position around this time and although the two concerns were run from Tonbridge, they remained independent until 1934 when the Festiniog had to bail out the unfortunate Welsh Highland, after the shareholders threatened to close the line.

At the time of the Colonel's appointment in early 1923 the Festiniog was a very interesting railway, for the Spooner concept of a narrow gauge main line railway still prevailed. Not that Colonel Stephens ever understood this for he waged a continual war on the management and staff of both North Wales lines for most of his latter years.

The locomotives and rolling stock were in good condition, although in some cases in need of overhaul, and the buildings, quite unlike the structures on the Colonel's other lines were constructed of sturdy local stone and slate. In the spirit of a main line the Festiniog was fully signalled with semaphores and disc-and-crossbar types. The permanent way was well kept and regularly relaid, using bullhead rail on cast chairs, unlike most other narrow-gauge lines which generally used flat bottomed rail and dog spikes. At the Blaenau Ffestiniog end of the line the Company had joint facilities with both the GWR and the LMS in addition to several yards connecting the various slate quarries in the district.

The line to Dinas, which had lost its passenger service in 1870, was still thriving with slate traffic. The workshops were at Boston Lodge, and were like a Swindon or Crewe, when compared with Rolvenden or Selsey, and were more than well equipped to handle the most difficult of repairs and overhauls.

All the day-to-day administration was carried out from Harbour Station and it was here that the resident line manager presided over the affairs of the FR Company and also later the Welsh Highland, in addition to his original responsibilities.

The locomotives during this period comprised an interesting mixture of 0-4-0STs rebuilt from the original George England locomotives, and the later development of 0-4-4-0 double Fairlie locomotives—not the sort of motive power common on a narrow-gauge light railway. In addition to this the railway had a fleet of bogie and four-wheel carriages, some of which were used only on quarrymen's trains, whereas the bogie vehicles operated on the through services from Porthmadog to Blaenau Ffestiniog.

The FR had a large fleet of goods vehicles ranging from covered vans and gunpowder vans to wooden open wagons and slate wagons. Most of the slate quarries had private fleets of vehicles, together with the GWR and LMS who had their own narrow-gauge slate wagons.

The Colonel was responsible for the introduction of internal combustion locomotives to the line shortly after his appointment in 1923. They were an armour-plated Simplex tractor, ex-War Department, purchased for use on shunting duties, and a gas-electric 0-4-0 locomotive from the American Army, built to a Baldwin design by the Pittsburgh Model Engineering Company. Both locomotives still operate on the Festiniog today, the Simplex being named *Mary Ann* and the Baldwin, rebuilt to a 2-4-0, is named *Moelwyn*.

The Festiniog suffered badly during the depression of the late 1920s and early 1930s, when road competition took away much of the local goods trade and a number of slate quarries closed down, although the summer tourist traffic still boomed, which helped the Company get over some of the financial problems. The Colonel was very autocratic and would often drop in at the wrong time to see how things were going. On these occasions the staff would quickly put their defensive plans into action. One early warning signal adopted by the locomotive drivers was to stroke their beards as the train carrying the Colonel pulled into each station; in this way the station staff knew he was on the train.

The Colonel always had an annual tour around Boston Lodge Works, during which he had all the working locomotives lined up in a row to inspect them. If he found anything wrong he would fly into a temper and make acid remarks about the defect and order the guilty individual to put it right immediately. On one occasion the Colonel referred to the fact that the locomotive inspection pits at Boston Lodge were so dirty and disgusting that a rat would think twice before jumping in and drowning in them. The Colonel would sometimes return to

Tonbridge and send a starchy memo outlining his grounds for displeasure. Most of the memos were thrown into the bin by the recipients, which made relations even worse. The Colonel was made Chairman and Managing Director of both the Festiniog and Welsh Highland in 1925. After he died in October 1931 the line passed into the hands of Mr Austen, who along with the Festiniog Board operated services until 16 September 1939 when all passenger trains ceased. The Company meanwhile had taken over the unfortunate Welsh Highland Railway in 1934, a move which helped to bankrupt the Festiniog Railway. The Railway operated a goods train service until late 1946 when all services were suspended. The line was left to nature until 1951 when a preservation society was formed to reopen the line, from Porthmadog to Blaenau Ffestiniog. The Railway now enjoys an ever-increasing summer traffic and slowly but surely over the last quarter century the new company has reopened the line, little by little back towards Blaenau Ffestiniog.

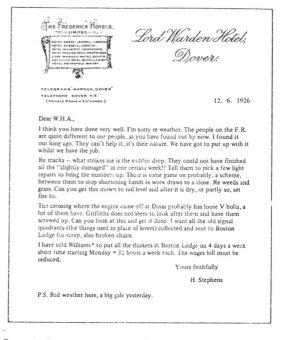

One of Colonel Stephens' letters to W. H. Austen regarding work standards on the Festiniog Railway.

Double Fairlie locomotive *Taliesin* and Porthmadog-bound train at Tan-y-Bwlch in the early 1930s. The train is made up of Festiniog bogie carriages and a short wheelbase brake third, next to the locomotive. At this time most of the carriage stock was painted green with black panelling, while locomotives were painted in unlined dark olive green. However, the front brake vehicle is in light brown livery. *Lens of Sutton*

Shunting slates at Blaenau Ffestiniog in 1920, with England saddle tank *Welsh Pony* built in 1867. The ornate green livery with its square panel lining dates from pre first world war days. In the station yard in the background is the LNWR goods shed and behind are the quarry inclines and slate tips.   *Ken Nunn LCGB*

Armour-plated ex-Light Railway Operations Department Simplex petrol rail tractor at Harbour Station in 1925, showing the controls, hand brake and the petrol tank on the far side of the driver's seat. This petrol tractor is still alive and well, and now named *Mary Ann.*
Real Photographs

A double Fairlie pounds towards Tan-y-Bwlch, through the steeply sided cutting approaching the station, with a train of mixed stock consisting of quarrymen's coaches known as bug boxes, and bogie vehicles.
Real Photographs

10 THE WELSH HIGHLAND RAILWAY (See map on page 62)
(Formerly the North Wales Narrow Gauge Railway)

The Welsh Highland Railway had its origins in the early 1870s when the Spooner family promoted the North Wales Narrow Gauge Railway which ran from Dinas, on the LNWR Afonwen-Caernarvon line, to Rhyd-ddu, later South Snowdon. The NWNGR had a branch which ran from Tryfan Junction to Bryngwyn but this lost its passenger service quite early in the line's history, on 15 August 1877.

The railway opened to traffic on 21 May 1877 and right from the beginning ran at a loss. The only time when any money could be made was when the tourists visited the area in the peak summer months. The Company carried on until just before the outbreak of world war I in August 1914. In December 1913 the passenger service had ceased over the whole line followed by complete closure to traffic of the line on the 31 October 1916. Much of the original rolling stock was sold for further use by military railways.

The line was then left derelict for five years, until, shortly after the war, Colonel Stephens surveyed the railway to ascertain its potential as a light railway. He also planned to extend the line south through Beddgelert and the Aberglaslyn Pass over part of the former Croesor Tramway to Porthmadog where it would join the Festiniog Railway.

Work commenced on the reconstruction of the NWNGR in late 1921 and the first stage of the new Company's line from Dinas to Beddgelert was opened on 31 July 1922. The railway changed its name from the North Wales Narrow Gauge Railway to the Welsh Highland Railway in July 1922. The final extension was commissioned on 1 June 1923, when the line was connected to the Festiniog at Porthmadog.

The Welsh Highland ran across the Cambrian line at Porthmadog and then down the High Street to Harbour Station, the Welsh Highland station being named Porthmadog New Station. The buildings along the new through line were a mixture of stone-built structures, as on the former NWNGR, and primitive corrugated-iron buildings, as at stations south of South Snowdon.

Porthmadog New Station was merely a collection of corrugated-iron buildings to the north of the Cambrian-Welsh Highland level crossing; at one stage the Festiniog and Welsh Highland trains ran from the New Station but this changed in the early 1930s when the FR reverted to Harbour Station.

The Welsh Highland's shed and workshop was situated at Dinas, although often locomotives were sent to Boston Lodge for heavy repairs.

Quite unlike the Festiniog, the Welsh Highland was not a main line narrow-gauge railway, and it is here that the Colonel misunderstood the whole concept of the Spooner principle. The Festiniog, and for that matter the North Wales Narrow Gauge Railway, were built not as light railways but as narrow gauge main lines, fully signalled, with sturdy earthworks and buildings. The Colonel could not grasp that both lines were designed to allow narrow-gauge trains to run at speeds higher than on some standard gauge branches; worse, he was very dogmatic about his way of doing things and even though the men of the Festiniog and WHR knew their jobs and ran their railways extremely well, he always knew better, which caused a great deal of criticism on both lines.

The Welsh Highland inherited two locomotives from the NWNGR, together with some goods rolling stock. Colonel Stephens added to this stock by purchasing an ex-War Department Baldwin 4-6-0T of the same class as the locomotives used on the Ashover and Snailbeach lines. This machine, which bore the number 590, was not a great success on the line and as the locomotive crews and shed staff disliked it intensely, the Baldwin was mostly used on goods trains, while the ex-NWNGR 0-6-4T *Moel Tryfan* and 2-6-2T *Russell* were used on passenger duties.

The original NWNGR coaches with Cleminson radial trucks had been replaced by a fleet of eleven bogie carriages, one of which was rebuilt as a buffet car in 1934. The goods vehicles varied from iron-built slate wagons and

Beddgelert on the Welsh Highland, with Festiniog Railway 0-4-0STT No 5 in the foreground about to leave for Portmadog, and WHR 2-6-2T *Russell* standing with a train from Dinas.

wooden open wagons borrowed from the FR to ex-Croesor Tramway open wagons and NWNGR vans.

Apart from tourism during the summer the line relied heavily on the few quarries in the Moelwyn area; however, their yield was far below that of the quarries at Blaenau Ffestiniog. The Welsh Highland had its administrative offices at Harbour Station on the Festiniog, but this situation changed in 1934, when, owing to pressure from shareholders, the Festiniog had to take over the Welsh Highland and operate it under a lease. The Welsh Highland, like its predecessor, had run at a loss almost from its opening in 1923 and this was a last chance to see whether anything could be done to put the books straight.

The original plan to allow Welsh Highland and Festiniog trains to run right through from Dinas to Blaenau Ffestiniog had long since gone and trains from both lines met at each side of the crossing at Porthmadog New Station. This arrangement changed yet again in 1935, when passengers had to walk through the town from Porthmadog New to the Harbour Station to catch their FR connection.

Over the years from 1923, the Colonel had experimented with internal combustion engined locomotives; however he did not find a satisfactory machine to replace the smaller 0-4 0STs used on the line, all of which were on loan from the Festiniog. The most successful locomotive was a Kerr Stuart Diesel-electric 0-6-0 which was on loan to the Company in the late 1920s; after trials the machine was sold to a sugar plantation in Mauritius, where one can still see it at work.

After two years under lease to the Festiniog

Railway it was decided to close the line, because there was no sign of financial improvement; the last passenger train ran on 26 September 1936, after which the passenger stock was stored at Dinas. The final goods train ran in May 1937 and after the departure of the last booked train, the rolling stock that remained was stored at Dinas and Beddgelert. Some stock which had been on loan had to be returned to the Festiniog. This was worked in a special train a short time after closure. Soon afterwards the crossing over the Cambrian, together with the signal cabin, was removed.

The remaining Welsh Highland rolling stock and equipment lay derelict; *Moel Tryfan* had been undergoing repair at Boston Lodge when closure took place, so the locomotive remained dismantled until cut up in 1954. Both *Russell* and the *Baldwin* were stored at Beddgelert goods shed. The Festiniog took over a number of former Welsh Highland carriages in 1936 and these vehicles are still running in a rebuilt form on the Festiniog Railway today.

The dismantling of the line took place during 1941 and early 1942, when the government requisitioned the whole undertaking for scrap metal to help the war effort. The railway was lifted in two halves, the first section from South Snowdon to Dinas, taking in the Bryngwn Branch which was completed in early 1942, and the southern portion from South Snowdon to Porthmadog New, which was completed in late 1941. In the early 1960s a Society was formed to try and re-open the line and their efforts seem to be slowly bearing fruit for they now own several locomotives and other vehicles including *Russell*, which after closure was sold to the Brymbo Steel Company and later resold to Pike Fayle & Company of Corfe Castle, Dorset. After this locomotive became redundant it was sold to the Birmingham Locomotive Club which stored it for some years at Towyn. Later the Welsh Highland Society took it over for future use on the line after restoration.

A train for Dinas runs through the Aberglaslyn pass, as a baby Austin with fabric top runs up the road from Porthmadog on the opposite side of the river. The train is made up of WHR stock and headed by an FR England 0-4-0ST.　　　　*Charles E. Lee collection*

A Dinas-bound train headed by *Russell* waits while Baldwin 590 enters Beddgelert Station with a train from Porthmadog New in the early 1930s. Already *Russell* has had its cab cut down and acquired a squat stove-pipe chimney. All these modifications were done during the abortive project to operate trains through from Dinas on the WHR to Blaenau Ffestiniog on the FR. In the picture can be seen the WHR bogie carriages in a variety of colours, for example, pink, bright yellow and green. Note also the ex-NWNGR observation car next to *Russell*.   *Lens of Sutton*

Baldwin 590 shunts WHR stock at Boston Lodge works in early 1936. The FR was very sophisticated in its operation compared with the WHR. Note the starting signal in background behind the Baldwin 4-6-0T. The WHR did not have signalling on the lower section relying on the staff and ticket principle and verbal instruction or handsignals throughout. However some semaphore signals were found on the former NWNGR section above Beddgelert.   *Lens of Sutton*

Porthmadog New Station in July 1935. *Russell* simmers with a Beddgelert-bound train, while the crew passes the time in chat. Porthmadog New was a very primitive station compared with the FR's Harbour Station. New Station consisted of a collection of corrugated iron huts forming a cafe, waiting room and station office. At one time Harbour Station was closed and both FR and WHR trains used this ill-equipped place; however this changed in the early 1930s when the FR went back to operating from Harbour Station.   *Real Photographs*

11 THE SNAILBEACH DISTRICT RAILWAYS

The Snailbeach District Railways were promoted and built to serve the lead mines in and around the Snailbeach and Stiperstones area of Shropshire. The scheme to build the line started in 1873, when under an Act of Parliament the construction of a mineral line was authorised between Pontesbury on the GWR/LNWR joint branch to Minsterley and Snailbeach. Extensions of the line were to be authorised after the first part had been built and these included a branch from Snailbeach to Pennerley and latterly an ambitious scheme, using the 1896 Light Railways Act, to build a line to Gratten Lodge from Perkins Beach. This line would of course include a branch from Pennerley to Gravels.

The first section from Pontesbury to Snailbeach was opened to traffic in July 1877 and from the start the Company had to struggle to make ends meet. The only extensions built along the line were from the main trunk point to various lead mines, the main branch being the line from Snailbeach to Stiperstones lead mine, which was opened shortly after the main line in 1877.

One of the main promoters of the line was Sir Henry Dyke Dennis of Glyn Valley Tramway fame. Indeed, in the early days of the Snailbeach, the 0-6-0 tram locomotive *Sir Theodore* had been on loan to the line for use in construction. However, the engine kept derailing because of the difference in gauge between the

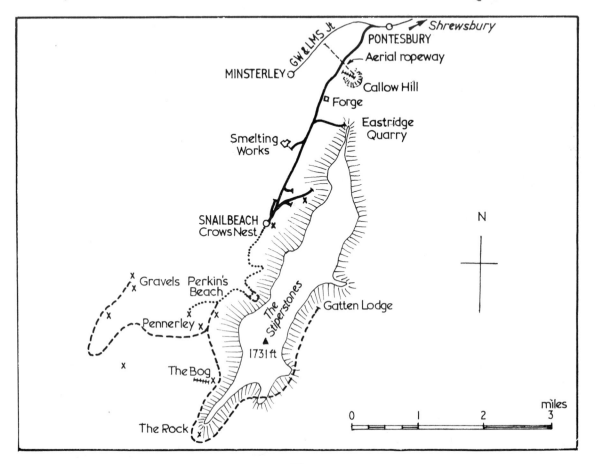

two lines, the GVT being 2ft 4¼in and the SDR 2ft 3¾in. Under the original management the line had three locomotives, an 0-6-0ST named *Fern Hill*, built in 1875, an 0-4-2ST named *Belmont* built by Hughes in 1873, and an 0-6-0T named *Dennis*, built by Bagnall in 1910.

The Snailbeach also had a large collection of open wagons. During the early part of the first world war the lead in the area was almost worked out but the line carried on until autumn 1915 when along with most of the mines the railway closed. The locomotives *Fernhill* and *Belmont* had been sent away to the GVT by the time of the 1915 closure, leaving only *Dennis* to work the line.

The railway was taken over by the Colonel in January 1923 and at the time of take over the whole concern was in a deplorable state. The Colonel took steps to improve matters, starting with permanent way which was relaid using heavier rail and new sleepers. He purchased 30 wagons from the War Department and three second-hand locomotives were obtained, two ex-War Department Baldwin 4-6-0Ts and the third being a *Skylark* class Kerr Stuart 0-4-2T, purchased from the Admiralty. From the reopening, the line earned much of its revenue from the quarries at Callow Hill, although there were several other sources of income.

The locomotive shed and workshop was situated at Stiperstones; here all rolling stock was repaired and overhauled.

The only original locomotive left after the Colonel's takeover was *Dennis*. He inspected this machine shortly after assuming control but he was not pleased with its condition and promptly ordered Driver Gatford, the Acting Shed Foreman, to overhaul her and get her back into traffic. However, Driver Gatford had other ideas; he hated the engine's guts and was determined not to overhaul or to operate her.

Over the next few years Gatford took *Dennis* apart very slowly. The Colonel on one occasion

Map of the Snailbeach District Railways: the solid line denotes No 1 railway actually constructed, the dotted line No 2 railway, which was not built, and the remainder the proposal under the 1896 Light Railways Act to extend from Perkins Beach to Gatten Lodge with a branch to Gravels; the crosses on the latter section represent lead mines.

even sent to Bagnalls for a copy of the drawings, which he later forwarded to Gatford in the hope that he would get weaving on the job. No such luck! Our friendly Acting Shed Foreman kept *Dennis* in bits from 1923 to 1936 when she was officially withdrawn. She was broken up slowly between 1937-1938.

The Colonel originally intended to operate passenger trains along the line, even going as far as to obtain land up to Pontesbury Station. Apart from surveying this section nothing more happened and the scheme was soon forgotten. The line bumbled along through the late 1920s and early 1930s and after the Colonel died in 1931, Austen took over the management but little changed.

The Colonel had given firm instructions that the locomotives were to be used in service for operating spells of two to three weeks only. This was good management at the time, but this order, which was adhered to long after his death, meant that all three of the operating locomotives wore out beyond repair at about the same time in 1950.

The traffic on the line ran down during the latter part of the second world war. This coupled with the fact that both the locomotives and track needed renewal made the railway uneconomic by 1946. All three locomotives were out of action with boiler defects and the Company had to use a Fordson farm tractor to tow the wagons along the line from Pontesbury to Snailbeach, the loaded vehicles being returned by gravity.

During 1947 Shropshire County Council took over the line under a lease together with the quarry at Callow Hill. The main trunk route south of Callow Hill became disused shortly after the Council take-over in 1947 and the locomotives were left to rust outside their shed at Stiperstones until the trackwork and derelict rolling stock were cleared by contractors in 1950. The northern section to Callow Hill remained in use until the autumn of 1959 when the County Council ceased to operate it. In 1961 a local scrap dealer lifted the remaining track and broke up the few remaining hopper wagons. The Tallyllyn Railway purchased some of the rail and points; however, none of the hopper wagons survived to be preserved.

Today there is still much to see of the line; narrow gauge track remains at Stiperstones near the locomotive shed, which still stands, and one can still walk the whole line from Pontesbury to Snailbeach.

nothing further to do with the railway even though he was a member of the Board of the old company.

The Great Western later rebuilt two bogie carriages to operate the line, in addition to which the railway was the preserve of the 2021 Class 0-6-0PTs in its later years. The railway was notable for its restricted loading gauge. which meant that even new bogie coaches built for the line by the GWR in 1939 had low almost flat arc roofs.

The line closed to passenger traffic on 20 September 1953. However, today a portion of the line is still open, from Llanelly, on the former GWR main line to Swansea, to Burry Port. Long may it survive to remind us of happier days.

Hudswell Clark 0-6-0T locomotive *Pioneer* at Burry Port in 1909 shortly after delivery from Leeds. The liveries of the BPGV locomotives varied from locomotive to locomotive; most of the Avonside Engineering 0-6-0STs were in lined green but the Hudswell Clark locomotives were painted unlined black with burnished brass work.
LPC Ian Allan

One of the BPGV 0-6-0 saddle tanks stands at Pontyberem Station with a train of Metropolitan rigid eight-wheelers.   *L&GRP*

Ponteberem and a train of ex-Metropolitan stock in 1909. The carriages consist of two Met third class rigid eight-wheelers and a Met six-wheeled carriage; at the back is a GWR four-wheeled brake van. The locomotive depicted here is now preserved at Didcot by members of the Great Western Society who intend eventually to restore it to BPGVR livery.   *LPC Ian Allan*

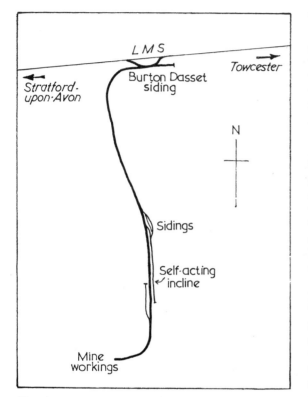

This line, built under contract by the Colonel for a private mineral company, was promoted shortly after the first world war, in 1920, to transport minerals from the newly opened ironstone mines at Edge Hill in Oxfordshire to the sidings at Burton Dassett where the light railway joined the Stratford-on-Avon & Midland Junction Railway, later part of the LMS.

A strange story surrounds the line for it appears that the original plans put forward by the line's promoters were dashed when the main seams of ironstone gave out soon after the line opened to traffic. However, the main seam of ironstone continued outside the boundaries of the mining company, but the private landowner objected to a scheme to continue mining on his land, and so in early 1924 the workings were closed down and the railway ceased to operate.

The Edge Hill Railway was a purely mineral line, and at no time were any passengers carried. The rolling stock consisted of two LBSC Terrier 0-6-0Ts, one of class A1 and the other an A1X, and a Manning Wardle 0-4-0 contractors' saddle tank, named *Sankey*. In addition to this the Company owned a collection of four-wheeled open wagons and two GER brake vans. After closure in 1925 the locomotives and rolling stock were left to rot until they were broken up along with the railway in 1947.

Abandoned stock at Edge Hill in 1945, including an ex LBSCR A1 0-6-0T, a Great Eastern Railway brake van and several four-wheeled open mineral wagons. The incline, which was rope worked, can be seen in the background. By this time the Edge Hill Railway was very desolate indeed, almost hidden from the world by weeds and dereliction.   *Lens of Sutton*

Manning Wardle 0-4-0ST *Sankey* would normally be found at the top of the incline at Edge Hill. It was stored under a road overbridge, like the other stock, which included two LBSCR 'Terriers', and a host of goods vehicles of various origins. After the line closed suddenly in the early 1920s *Sankey* was left to rot until it was cut up in 1946 with the rest of the rolling stock.
L&GRP

Edge Hill 0-6-0T No 1, formerly LBSCR No 73 *Deptford.* Although this engine, seen here in 1930s, had been out of use for some years it was not scrapped until 1946.
L&GRP

14 THE NORTH DEVON & CORNWALL JUNCTION RAILWAY

The North Devon & Cornwall Junction Railway was the last standard gauge line to be constructed by the Colonel. The railway ran from Torrington, on the Southern's branch to Bude, to Halwill Junction on the Southern's branch to Wadebridge. The railway was constructed by an independent company in much the same way as the Sheppey Light Railway. This scheme was put into effect partly to relieve unemployment in the West Country in the early 1920s.

It was opened to traffic on 27 July 1925 and from the opening the Southern Railway operated the line on behalf of the Company.

However the line was never owned by the Southern Railway, and did not become part of the Southern system proper until after nationalisation in 1948, when it was taken into the Southern Region. In 1963 all Southern Region lines west of Salisbury were handed over to the Western Region which closed it on 1 March 1965 to passenger traffic, but the line is still open to Meeth for china clay traffic.

The North Devon & Cornwall line incorporated part of the 3ft gauge Torrington & Marland Mineral Tramway. The station buildings along the line were very similar to those on the K&ESR, and were constructed of corrugated iron and wood, although some were built of local stone. Motive power was in the form of rebuilt E1R 0-6-2Ts which had been specially reconstructed by R. E. L. Maunsell at Eastleigh for operating in the West of England and O2 0-4-4Ts working rail motor sets. Later this changed to LMR type Ivatt 2-6-2Ts and corridor stock.

The line served the farming community of the north western part of Devon and Cornwall and, like most rural lines of its type, it was a victim of the Beeching Plan in the early 1960s.

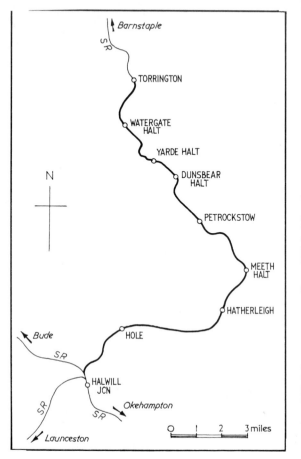

Top:
A Torrington & Marland Mineral Railway train crosses a timber trestle near Marland in 1912. This 3ft gauge line was built in 1880 to connect various quarries with the jetty at Torrington; the locomotive is an 0-6-0ST and the train consists of empty four-wheeled short-wheelbase open wagons. The tramway was later converted to standard gauge by Colonel Stephens in 1923.
Author's collection

Right:
A Class E1R 0-6-2T and an ex LSWR push-pull coach cross a viaduct near Torrington in 1935. The photograph shows the construction of the brick and steel girder bridge. *LCGB Ken Nunn collection*

JUNCTION RAILWAY

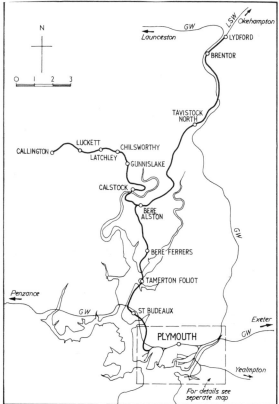

The Plymouth, Devonport & South Western Junction Railway, Callington section, was opened to traffic on 2 March 1908. The line, which had been promoted privately by an independent company outside the LSWR, ran from Bere Alston to Callington. However, the Company was on very good terms with the Board of the LSWR from the opening and trains had running rights between Bere Alston and Plymouth.

The section of line from the northern end of Calstock Viaduct to Gunnislake was built on the alignment of the former East Cornwall Mineral Railway, formerly a 3ft 6in gauge mineral tramway, opened in 1872 and which at one time served the local tin mines in the area. The East Cornwall line was taken over in 1894. During the time of the PD&SWJR's construction most of the mineral line was abandoned. The PD&SWJR served the tin mining and quarrying industries of the Tamar Valley, most of the traffic from which was channelled through Calstock where a wagon lift was built on to the

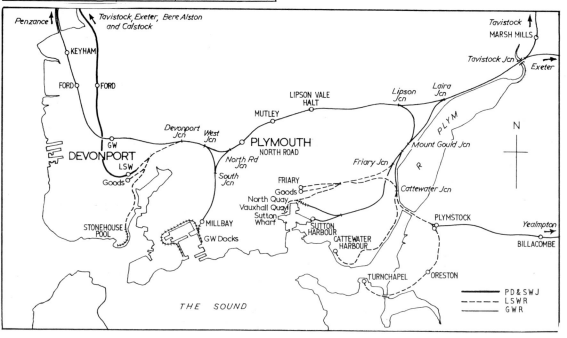

viaduct to serve the wharves from the main line.

According to Colonel Stephens, Calstock Viaduct over the Tamar was as deep in its foundations as it was in its height. He served the Company as engineer of works during construction of the line, and after the line's opening in 1908, he became the Company's resident manager. One of the stipulations of the Colonel's contract stated that in order to hold down the position he should be on hand for three days of the week to supervise the line's operation. As he was hardly ever on hand to do his job, the Board asked him to resign only a year after the line had opened.

The line became a part of the LSWR in early 1922, and was grouped into the Southern a year later. Things did not change much during Southern days, but a number of changes took place after nationalisation in 1948, when permanent way and signalling were renewed; in 1958 the line became part of the Western Region. Part of the line, from Gunnislake to Callington, was closed on 5 November 1966, leaving the section from Bere Alston to Gunnislake still open to passenger traffic, and indeed today providing the only passenger service on the former LSWR route out of Plymouth.

The railway had a handsome stud of three Hawthorn Leslie tank locomotives, of which two were 0-6-2Ts of a design not unlike K&ESR No 4 *Hecate*, in their body outline. The third machine was an 0-6-0T, again not unlike a K&ESR 2-4-0 in its outline. All three were named, the 0-6-2Ts being *Earl of Mount Edgcumbe* and *Earl St Leven*, the 0-6-0T receiving the name *A. S. Harris*.

The Company owned a fourth locomotive in the early days of the line, a former East Cornwall Mineral Railway 0-4-0ST converted from 3ft 6in gauge to standard gauge. This machine was used to shunt the yard at Callington but was later sold to Colonel Stephens for use on the Selsey Tramway along with the two former LSWR royal saloons, one of which went to the K&ESR and the other to the Shropshire & Montgomeryshire line.

The passenger rolling stock consisted of a set of eight North London Railway four-wheeled vehicles, which were replaced after a number of years with LSWR vehicles. A six-wheeled goods brake van was unusual for it incorporated a passenger compartment for quarry workers.

After the Southern takeover in 1923, the four-wheelers were replaced with LSWR gate push-pull trailers. The 0-6-0T *A. S. Harris* went far from home, among other places to Clapham Junction and Ashford. It was replaced by an O2

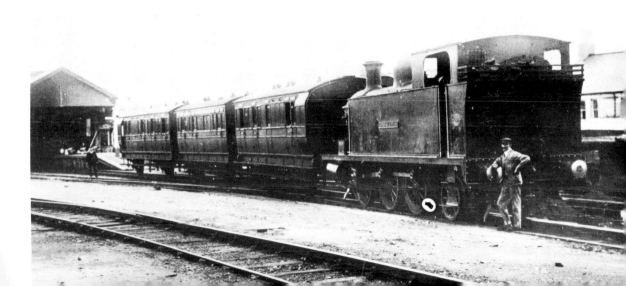

Earl St Leven at the head of a train of ex-LSWR four-wheeled coaches at Callington in 1911; in the background is the train shed. At this time a local train service was run between Callington and Calstock, in addition to trains for Bere Alston and Plymouth.
Lens of Sutton

0-4-4T on passenger trains. The 0-6-2Ts however remained in the district until the mid-1950s when they went to Eastleigh Works for scrapping, being replaced by Ivatt 2-6-2Ts of LMS design.

The station buildings along the line were very similar to Tenterden Town Station in design, except that in some cases the buildings were on island platforms with awnings at each side. At Callington there was a train shed which covered most of the platform.

The erstwhile PD&SWJR is now the furthest west that can be reached on the former Southern system. One of the main reasons for the retention of the last portion of the line is that the railway provides a lifeline across the River Tamar since there are no direct main roads between Gunnislake, Calstock and Plymouth. For the moment therefore the line continues to operate as a basic railway, in almost modern Stephens form.

Plymouth, Devonport & South Western Junction Railway locomotives at Callington shed in 1909, showing *Earl of Mount Edgcumbe*. At the head of two open wagons behind, *Earl St Leven* can be seen in the engine shed. The locomotives were painted blue at this time, but later the livery changed to a style similar to that used on the LSWR. *LPC Ian Allan*

Calstock viaduct shortly after the opening of the line in 1908 showing the wagon lift on the far left, which served an industrial complex on the west bank of the Tamar. *W. H. Austen collection TRC*

Bottom right:
A general view of Gunnislake Station in Southern Railway days showing the island platform and goods yard. Today with the bare minimum of facilities it is the terminus of a service from Plymouth and is the only one of the former Colonel Stephens' lines which came into the BR network to retain a passenger service. *L&GRP*

16 THE SHEPPEY LIGHT RAILWAY

The Sheppey Light Railway was constructed by the Colonel on behalf of an independent company. The line was opened to traffic on 1 August 1901, and ran from Queenborough on the SE&CR's Sheerness-Port Victoria branch to Leysdown on the east coast of the Island.

From the opening, the line was operated by the South Eastern & Chatham on the Company's behalf. Motive power was normally provided in the form of a Kitson rail motor, or for goods traffic an ex-LBSCR A1 0-6-0T purchased secondhand by the SE&CR for working the line. In the years after the SE&CR assumed control on 31 October 1905 the line was operated using class P 0-6-0T and R1 0-4-4Ts, coupled to auto trailers or converted former railmotor carriages articulated in pairs.

The station buildings along the line were very much like buildings on the Colonel's other railways and were constructed of corrugated iron with wood framing. The line made very little money for the original company, and still less for the SE&CR. Even though the railway was a white elephant the Southern continued to run the line through its time and it was not finally closed until 3 December 1950, only three years after nationalisation.

Eastchurch Station in 1950, showing the building and track layout. The building is a typical example of a Colonel Stephens' corrugated iron structure, with its extended awning and supports using v-shaped joints at the top. Note the gas lamps on the station platform and the concrete platform facing.   *Lens of Sutton*

84

SECR railcar No 1, shortly after being outshopped in 1901 and used from the early days of the line. These rail motors were withdrawn just before the first world war, the carriage portions being converted for normal locomotive working as push-pull sets, some articulated in pairs. *BR*

17 THE PADDOCKWOOD & HAWKHURST RAILWAY

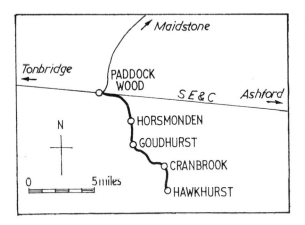

The Paddockwood & Hawkhurst Railway was the Colonel's first project at the early age of 22. The line was originally intended as a branch to connect Paddockwood to Rye, for which plans were made in 1845; however, nothing came of this first scheme, and other projects of a similar nature were put forward in the following years until 1864 when the South Eastern Railway, concerned over its position in the area, supported local promoters to project a line from Paddockwood to Cranbrook. At this time also a

separate company was formed to build a line from Cranbrook to Tenterden.

Work started on the line's construction in 1879 but soon stopped for financial reasons. After a short period the South Eastern Railway assumed control of the company but little happened until work started in earnest in 1891 with Stephens in charge of every aspect of construction. On 1 October 1892, the line was opened as far as Hope Mill, later renamed Goudhurst. This was followed a year later on 4 September by the continuation to Hawkhurst.

The railway was projected as a private local company which handed over the line to the South Eastern Railway on completion of the works. The main traffic was fruit and hops, which were transported to London from most stations. Most stations were some distance from the villages they served which did not help the line as far as passenger traffic was concerned. The route was difficult in some respects; the gradients were steep between Goudhurst and Cranbrook, the steepest being 1 in 60, and the line boasted a short tunnel near Cranbrook. The branch had a very uneventful life but had quite a variety of motive power during its time. In South

Eastern days Cudworth 2-4-0s and other small types were used; in Southern days a number of SECR and LBSCR locomotives were seen on the branch, among them Chatham R1 0-4-4Ts, SEC H Class 0-4-4Ts, C Class 0-6-0s, Brighton E1 0-6-0Ts and E4 0-6-2Ts. Even Brighton C2X 0-6-0s were tried for a short time, and surprisingly, larger classes of 4-4-0 tender locomotives were used as well, mostly on weekend excursion traffic.

The station buildings were quite interesting for they varied tremendously. Goudhurst was a substantial brick building, while Horsmonden and Hawkhurst stations were typical Colonel Stephens' corrugated-iron buildings. Cranbrook was a brick and timber structure of a plainer pattern when compared with Goudhurst. The line never really made a profit and it was not surprising that towards the later 1950s, British Railways took the first steps towards closure.

Branch train formations had remained much the same since early Southern days, with 0-4-4Ts working push-pull sets, and the occasional school specials using main line corridor stock, and the hop pickers' trains.

A Class C 0-6-0 works a pick-up freight near Cranbrook in early June 1961. The Hawkhurst branch handled a large proportion of the local fruit and hop traffic until closure in June 1961. Other classes used on the line at this time varied from H Class 0-4-4Ts to L1 4-4-0 tender locomotives. *D. Cobbe collection*

The line's final closure came on 6 June 1961, the same day as the neighbouring Kent & East Sussex branch. The last train was an enthusiasts' special, organised by the LCGB. However it was a number of years before contractors lifted the track and demolished the works. Today little is left to provide reminders of the branch, for most of the station buildings have gone and little remains of the course of the line.

Hawkhurst Station in 1956 showing the corrugated iron station building typical of Stephens' designs with the wooden supports under the awning. The gas lamps are quite ornate with their twirly main castings and the station name in the glass above the lantern. Note the tight run-round loop which could accommodate an L1 4-4-0; the carriages in the bay are former LSWR corridor vehicles some of which were originally used for emigrant traffic. Later they were converted for local push-pull workings by the Southern Railway. *Lens of Sutton*

18 THE PETROL RAILBUSES

The Wolseley Sidley being unloaded at Chichester on the Selsey Tramway about 1920. The car ran on this line coupled to a rail lorry. Later, after being involved in an accident, it was laid aside and then sent to Kinnerley on the S&M where its body was used to refurbish the trailer for *Gazelle*.   *E. C. Griffith*

The Wolseley Sidley chassis before the fitting of the railcar body at Rolvenden about 1919. Later a body was built by Drake & Fletcher of Maidstone. At this time the vehicle was used as a goods tractor.

F. H. Smith collection

Railbus luggage trolley at Rolvenden in 1947, used at this time for ballasting track by PW staff.

J. Norris collection

Above:
The second K&ESR Ford railbus set at Tenterden in 1928. It was delivered in 1924, supplied by Edmonds of Thetford, and sold in the late 1920s. The remaining railbus sets were withdrawn at the end of the 1930s and sold for scrap in 1941.   *J. E. Kite collection*

Top left:
The interior of the 1923 Ford set at Tenterden Station in 1924 showing the tramcar type slatted seats and sliding door between the two saloons. A steel hinged plate connected the two vehicles.
                W. H. Austen collection TRC

Above:
The Muir Hill tractor, at Clevedon in the late 1930s. This machine was the second shunting locomotive supplied by this firm, looking more like a garden shed on wheels, than a locomotive. It was used on the Wick St Lawrence branch to shunt goods vehicles on the concrete pier.   *W. H. Austen collection TRC*

Below:
The 50hp big Drewry railcar which was purchased from the Southern Railway in 1934, where it had operated on the Lydd branch on trials. The railcar operated on the WC&PR until closure in 1940, after which it was cut up. The compartment next to the nearest cab was for the conveyance of milk churns.   *H. C. Casserley*

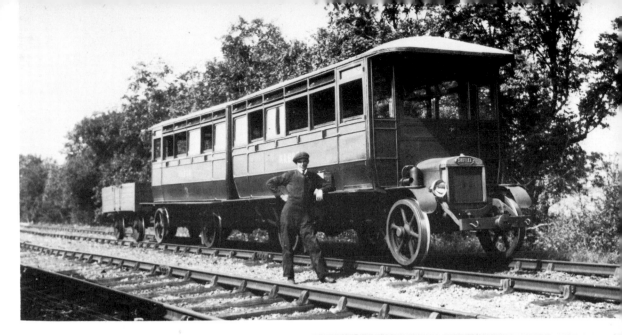

The K&ESR Shefflex set at Headcorn in 1934. It had been delivered in 1930 and was used extensively over the line until 1938 when it was withdrawn and sold in 1941.   *H. C. Casserley*

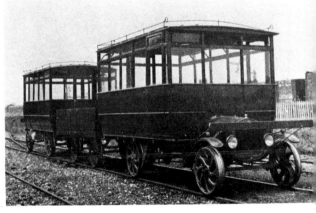

Ex-works at Chichester on the Selsey tramway in 1923, a Ford two-car set and luggage trolley. This set worked on the line until the end of services in 1935. Later a Shefflex two-car set was also purchased to supplement service on the line. Note the chilled cast wheels with shaped spokes.   *W. H. Austen TRC*

The S&M three-car set of 1923 here seen in ex-works condition. Contrary to popular belief the chassis of this set was not built by Fords, but a subsidiary American company under contract from Ford during the first world war. The set ran as a three-car unit for a time in the early 1920s after which it became a two-car set until 1933 when the line closed to passenger traffic. It was broken up in late 1935 at Kinnerley.

W. H. Austen TRC

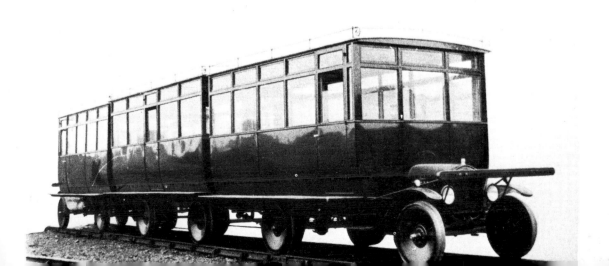

Above:
PD&SWJR 0-6-2T *Earl of Mount Edgcumbe* at Callington in 1908. Unlike the other Hawthorn tanks so far described this engine and its sister were fitted with Belpaire fireboxes. Both PD&SWJR 0-6-2Ts survived well into BR days and latterly in the late 1950s operated at Eastleigh works on shunting duties.

W. H. Austen collection

Bottom right:
S&M 0-6-2T at Kinnerley in 1912, one of two 0-6-2Ts purchased by the Colonel for the S&M. Later, just before the outbreak of the first world war both 0-6-2Ts were sold to the Woolmer Instructional Military Railway, later the Longmoor Military Railway.

LPC Ian Allan

Below:
PD&SWJR 0-6-0T *A. S. Harris*, here seen at Nine Elms in 1934. This engine was purchased to operate the passenger service on the PD&SWJR. However, after the Southern takeover in 1923 the locomotive soon moved to the London area where it worked as a shed and carriage pilot.

H. C. Casserley

Top right:
Rother Valley Railway 2-4-0T No 2 *Northiam* of 1899 at Rolvenden Shed in 1906, showing the locomotive with its original chimney before the stovepipe was fitted. Later, sister locomotive No 1 *Tenterden* was rebuilt with 4ft 1in driving wheels, purchased, it is believed, from the SE&CR. Both engines operated until the late 1930s when they were withdrawn and later sold for scrap, No 2 meanwhile, as mentioned earlier, having been in the Will Hay film, *Oh, Mr Porter.*   *W. H. Austen collection*

19   THE COLONEL'S HAWTHORNS

Right:
K&ESR 0-8-0T No 4 *Hecate*, built in 1904 for use on through trains over the main line between Headcorn and Tonbridge. This service never materialised, and as far as can be ascertained *Hecate* was used only once a year, during Biddenden fair week, to move the large amount of cattle traffic. In 1932 the KESR arranged an exchange with the Southern Railway for LSWR 0-6-0ST No 335 and two spare boilers. In Southern and early BR days *Hecate* worked from Nine Elms on carriage shunting duties at Clapham Junction until it was scrapped in 1950.   *W. H. Austen collection*

Railway	Gauge and distance	Location	Chronology	Traction
East Kent Rly	Standard main line 11¼ miles Branch 3½miles	Sheperdswell to Canterbury Road. Branch from Eastry to Sandwich Road.	Opened 1912. Closed 1951.	Steam
Rother Valley Rly Kent & East Sussex Rly	Standard 21¼ miles	Robertsbridge to Headcorn	Opened 1900 Closed 1961	Steam Petrol Diesel (BR)
Selsey Tramway, West Sussex Rly	Standard 7¾miles	Chichester to Selsey Beach	Opened 1897 Closed 1935	Steam Petrol
Shropshire & Montgomery-shire Light Rly	Standard	Shrewsbury to Llanymynech	Opened Potteries, Shrewsbury & North Wales Rly 1866. Closed 1880, re-opened as S&M 1911. Closed to passenger traffic 6.11.33. Army takeover 1941. Closed to all traffic 29.2.60	Steam Petrol Diesel (WD)
Weston Clevedon & Portishead Light Rly	Standard 14¼ miles	Weston Super Mare to Portishead	Opened 1897 Closed 1940	Steam Petrol
Ashover Light Rly	60cm 7¼ miles	Clay Cross Ashover	Opened 7.4.25 Closed 31.3.50 Passenger traffic ceased 30.9.36	Steam Petrol Diesel
Rye & Camber Tramway	3ft 2½miles	Rye to Camber Sands	Opened 1895 Closed 1939	Steam Petrol
Festiniog Rly	60cm 14¼ miles	Porthmadog to Blaenau Ffestiniog	Opened 1836. Closed 1943. Reopened 1951. To reopen to Blaenau Ffestiniog shortly.	Horse 1837-1888. Steam from 1888 to present day. 1920 petrol

Locomotive stock at closure or end of independent existence (list does not include motive power of subsequent operators or owners of lines ie SR or BR, or the FR and KESR as preserved)	Bibliography reference	Notes	Society Address
No 2　0-6-0, Ex-SR No 1383 No 4　0-6-0T, Kerr Stuart No 3067/17 No 6　0-6-0, Ex-SECR No 372 · No 1371 0-6-0, Ex-SR No 1371 Above locomotives vested·in the Railway Executive, 1 January 1948.	1, 6	One of the first. lines closed by BR	
No 3 0-6-0T, Ex-LBSCR No 670 No 4 0-6-0, Ex-LSWR No 0335 Above locomotives vested in the Railway Executive, 1 January 1948. (Southern Railway 0-6-0 No 3440 and 0-6-0T No 2678 were on loan at 31.12.1947).	1, 8	Reopened 1972	Tenterden Rly Co; Tenterden Station, Tenterden, Kent
No 3 *Chichester,* 0-6-0ST Hudswell, Clark, 1903 No 4 *Morous,* 0-6-0ST Manning Wardle, 1866 No 5 *Ringing Rock,* 0-6-0ST Manning Wardle, 1883			
No 1 *Gazelle* 0-4-2T Dodman, King's Lynn, 1893 No 8108 0-6-0, Ex-LMS No 8108 (LNWR built 1873) No 8182 0-6-0 Ex-LMS No 8182 (LNWR built 1873) No 8236 0-6-0 Ex-LMS No 8236 (LNWR built 1873) All above vested in the Railway Executive, 1 January 1948	1, 13		
No 1 *Clevedon* 2-4-0T Dubs & Co, 1875 No 2 *Portishead* 0-6-0T Ex-LBSCR No 643 No 3 *Weston* 0-6-0T No 4　0-6-0T Ex-SR No 2653 No 5　0-6-0T Manning Wardle No 1970/19 Also: two Drewry railcars 　　one Muir Hill Fordson petrol tractor Line closed 18 May 1940 — locomotives Nos 2 and 4 transferred to Great Western Railway, as Nos 5 and 6, which passed into BR ownership	1, 5	Taken into GWR in 1940	
Joan, 4-6-0T, Baldwin, USA, No 44720/17 *Peggy,* 4-6-0T, Baldwin, USA, No 44743/17 *Hummy,* 4-6-0T, Baldwin, USA, No 44370/17 　　40hp diesel. Planet No 3307/48	7, 3		
2-4-0T, W. G. Bagnall No 1461/95 Petrol locomotive. Kent Engineering Co (scrapped 1946) One carriage underframe preserved by NGRS at Brockham, Surrey.	3		
Line still open and under operation in association with Festiniog Railway Society. Locomotive stock at closure in 1946 was: No 1 *Princess*　0-4-0T No 2 *Prince*　0-4-0T No 3 *Taliesin*　0-4-4-0T No 4 *Palmerston* 0-4-0T No 5 *Welsh Pony* 0-4-0T No 10 *Merddin Emrys* 0-4-4-0T No 11　Petrol locomotive No 101　Simplex No 507/17	2, 10	Reopened 1955	Festiniog Rly Co, Harbour Stn, Porthmadog, Gwynedd

Railway	Gauge and distance	Location	Chronology	Traction
Welsh Highland Rly	60cm 7¼ miles	Dinas Jc to Porthmadog	Opened North Wales Narrow Gauge Rly 1877. closed 1916, reopened as Welsh Highland Rly 1922, closed to all traffic 1937. Bryngwyn branch closed to passengers 1877	Steam Petrol Diesel
Snailbeach District Rly	2ft 4in 3¼ miles	Pontesbury to Stiperstones Mine	Opened 1873. Closed 1915. Reopened 1922. Closed 1947	Steam
Burry Port & Gwendraeth Valley Rly	Standard 21 miles	Burry Port to Cwm Mawr (Carmarthenshire)	Opened 1869. Closed 1909 for rebuilding. Closed to passengers 1953	Steam
Edge Hill Light Rly	Standard 2¾ miles	Burton Drassett to Edge Hill Mine	Opened 1920. Closed 1925. Rly dismantled 1947	Steam
North Devon & Cornwall Junction Rly	Standard 20½ miles	Torrington to Halwill Junction	Opened 1922. Closed 1965. Absorbed by S R 1923 Section to Peters Marland still open to goods.	Steam Diesel (BR)
Plymouth, Devonport & South Western Junction Rly	Standard	Devonport dockyard to Callington via joint line as far as Bere Alston	Opened 1908	Steam Diesel (BR)
Isle of Sheppey Light Rly	Standard 8¾ miles	Queenborough to Leysdown	Opened 1905 Closed 1950	Steam
Hawkhurst Branch	Standard 7½ miles	Paddock Wood to Hawkhurst	Opened 1892/3 Closed 1961	Steam

Locomotive stock at closure or end of independent existence (list does not include motive power of subsequent operators or owners of lines ie SR or BR, or the FR and KESR as preserved)	Bibliography reference	Notes	Society Address
No 11 *Moel Tryfan*, 0-6-4T Vulcan Foundry, 1877 No 12 *Russell*, 2-6-2T Hunslet Engine Co No 901/06 No 590 4-6-0T Baldwin, USA, No 45172/17 Stock incorporated with Festiniog Railway, 1936. Nos 11 and 590 broken up at Boston Lodge Works. No 12 sold to Hook Norton Ironstone Co, Oxfordshire	7, 3	Society trying to reopen line from northern end	
No 2, 0-4-2-T, Kerr Stuart No 802/1901 No 3, 4-6-0T, Baldwin, USA, No 44383/16 No 4, 4-6-0T, Baldwin, USA, No 44522/17 All cut-up 1950	4, 14		
Locomotives taken into GWR stock, 1923: No 1 *Ashburnham* 0-6-0ST. Chapman & Furneaux No 1197. (GWR No 2192) No 2 0-6-0T. Hudswell, Clark No 1066. (GWR No 2162) No 3 *Burry Port* 0-6-0ST. Chapman & Furneaux No 1209. (GWR No 2193) No 4 *Kidwelly* 0-6-0ST. Avonside Engine Co No 1463. (GWR No 2194) No 5 *(Cwm Mawr)* 0-6-0ST. Avonside Engine Co No 1491. (GWR No 2195) No 6 *Gwendraeth* 0-6-0ST. Avonside Engine Co No 1519. (GWR No 2196) No 7 *(Pembrey)* 0-6-0ST. Avonside Engine Co No 1535. (GWR No 2176) No 8 *Pioneer* 0-6-0T. Hudswell, Clark No 871. (GWR No 2197) No 9 0-6-0T. Hudswell, Clark No 893. (GWR No 2163) No 10 0-6-0T. Hudswell Clark No 924. (GWR No 2198) No 11 0-6-0T. Hudswell, Clark No 969. (GWR No 2164) No 12 0-6-0T. Hudselll, Clark No 1024. (GWR No 2165) No 13 0-6-0T. Hudswell, Clark No 1222. (GWR No 2166) No 14 0-6-0T. Hudswell, Clark No 1385. (GWR No 2167) No 15 0-6-0T. Hudswell, Clark No 1164. (GWR No 2168) All except GWR Nos 2163/4 passed to British Railways	1, 18	Taken into GWR in 1923	
No 1 0-6-0T. Ex-LBSCR No 673 No 2 0-6-0T. Ex-LBSCR No 674 *Sankey* 0-4-0ST. Manning Wardle All cut-up 1946	4, 15		
No stock Worked at various time by locomotives of LDSCR, LSWR, SR, BR(I MR) steam types and by BR diesel locomotives.	1, 11	Part of track bed formerly a section of the Torrington & Marland 3ft gauge tramway	
No 3 *A S Harris*. 0-6-0T. Hawthorn Leslie No 2695/07 No 4 *Earl of Mount Edgcumbe*. 0-6-2T. Hawthorn Leslie No 2697/07 No 5 *Lord St Leven*. 0-6-2T. Hawthorn Leslie No 2696/07 Became Southern Railway Nos 756, 757 and 758 respectively and passed into British Railways stock as Nos 30756-8. Line also worked by LSWR O2 0-4-4T and BR (LMR) 2-6-2T. Currently worked by BR diesels and diesel multiple units	1	Line as far as Gunnislake still open. Track bed on part of East Cornwall mineral railway 3ft 6in gauge	
No stock. Worked by SECR locomotives	1	Worked and later owned by SE&CR	
No stock Worked by SECR, LBSCR locomotives	17		

Fortunately not all the Colonel Stephens' lines have gone and one of the most important, the Kent & East Sussex, has been revived by a 'preservation society which now runs tourist passenger trains over part of the former Rother Valley section from Tenterden towards Northiam, and ultimately Bodiam. Moreover, former LBSCR Terrier 0-6-0Ts, which characterised so many of Colonel Stephens' railways, can still be seen in action, as here with present day Tenterden Railway Company No 10 on a works train in 1976.   *Tim Stephens*

Acknowledgements

I should like to thank the following people and organisations for their help in compiling information for this volume:
The Tenterden Railway Company; Custodians of the W. H. Austen collection of photographs and data; Ian Allan (for LPC Photographs); the Locomotive Club of Great Britain for the Ken Nunn collection; Lens of Sutton; Gregory Pictures; Mr Childs of the Clay Cross Company; Punch Magazine; Real Photographs Co; W. H. Austen; J. Norris; F. H. Smith; D. A. Boreham; I. Gotheridge; H. C. Casserley; Charles E. Lee; E. C. Griffith; D. Cobbe; D. Kevann; P. Lemmey; J. E. Kite and M. Williams.

I should like to give special acknowledgement to Robert Inns who through thick and thin has helped me by producing copies from old historic photographs of excellent quality, often at times from very poor originals; also at this point I should like to pay tribute to the late Charles Kentsley who throughout his lifetime supported preservation and documentation of all railways large and small. Without Charles' backing and enthusiasm I doubt whether I should have started researching the railways of Colonel Stephens and hence written this account. It is a great shame that he did not live to see the volume published.

Bibliography

Oakwood Press Books:
1-4 *Light Railway Handbooks* 1, 2, 3, 5.
5   *The Weston, Clevedon and Portishead Light Railway* by C. Maggs.
6   *The East Kent Railway* by A. R. Catt.
7   *The Ashover Light Railway* by K. Plant.
8   *The Kent & East Sussex Railway by* S. Garratt.
9   *The Plymouth, Devonport & South Western Junction Railway* by A. J. Cheesman.
10 *Festiniog Railway* Vols 1 and 2 by J. I. C. Boyd.
11 *Southern Branches in the 1930s* by R. W. Kidner.
12 *The Welsh Highland Railway* by Charles E. Lee, David & Charles.

Industrial Railway Society Books:
13 *The Shropshire & Montgomeryshire Light Railway* by E. Tonks.
14 *Snailbeach District Railway* by E. Tonks.
15 *The Edge Hill Light Railway* by E. Tonks.
16 *The Selsey Tramway* by E. C. Griffith, published privately.
17 *The Hawkhurst Railway* by R. W. Crombleholme.
18 Great Western Railway Magazine.
19 Welsh Highland Railway Society Publications.